T0159909

The
REBIRTH
of
BUDDHA

IRH PRESS

BOOKS
IRH PRESS
New York

ISBN 13: 978-1-942125-95-2
ISBN 10: 1-942125-95-X
Cover Image: topimages / Shutterstock.com
Vensto / Shutterstock.com
Angvara Photo / Shutterstock.com
suraphol boonyavannakul / Shutterstock.com

Printed in Canada

First Edition

The
REBIRTH
of
BUDDHA

RYUHO OKAWA

再仏
誕陀

MY ETERNAL DISCIPLES,
HEAR MY WORDS

IRH Press

Contents

CHAPTER ONE

Now, Here, I Have Returned

CHAPTER TWO

Words of Wisdom

CHAPTER THREE
Do Not Be Foolish

CHAPTER FOUR

Politics and Economics

CHAPTER FIVE

Patience and Success

CHAPTER SIX

What Is Reincarnation?

CHAPTER SEVEN

Faith and the Road to Creating Buddha Land

Preface to the New Edition

About 2,500 years ago, on Vulture Peak in India, overlooking Rajagriha, the capital of the Magadha Kingdom, I would give sermons to my disciples. That deep emotion comes back to my heart.

At that time, with shaved heads and in saffron robes, you were weeping for joy at my sermons. Now, you are born into a different age, in a different country, wearing different clothes.

However, your heart that feels Buddha's Truth must be the same.

Master and disciples are eternally tied by the Laws. The Buddha, Dharma, and Sangha are one.

This eternal book is my gift for you again.

Ryuho Okawa
Master & CEO of Happy Science Group
October 1994

Preface (Original Edition)

As you can see in each chapter, this book, *The Rebirth of Buddha*, describes the core teachings of Buddhism in the form of a message from Shakyamuni Buddha in his own words to his disciples. For this reason, this book will be a sure guide to those who have awakened to Buddha's Truth, and at times, it will be a stern warning to them.

Many people may have studied Buddhism, but I think there has never been a time when the essence of Buddhism has been taught as straightforwardly as in this book. Because it is taught as a direct message, it is easy to understand and gets right to the heart of the teachings.

This book is a must-have for all of you who undergo spiritual training. You must always keep it at hand. I am earnestly hoping that you savor it to the end.

Ryuho Okawa
Master & CEO of Happy Science Group
July 1989

CHAPTER ONE

Now, Here, I Have Returned

All of you, my disciples,
Do you remember my voice?
You must have heard me speak long ago.
For tens of thousands of years,
Hundreds of thousands, or even millions of years,
You have been born on earth with me.
And in the Real World too,
You have continued to learn the Path as my disciples.

Awaken

All of you, my disciples,
Now, here, I have returned.
Be delighted at my rebirth.
Notice my rebirth.
Awaken to my rebirth, to this fact, to this time.

Far in the past, in the land of India,
You must have heard me speak.
Thousands or tens of thousands of my eternal disciples,
Who heard my teachings in the land of India—
You must awaken.

Are you still indulging yourself in deep sleep?
How can I start my true work
When you remain asleep?
When I awaken,
All my disciples must awaken as well.
When I speak,
All my disciples must gather to me.

My eternal disciples,
Hear this dear sound.
Hear this dear voice.
Remember these dear words from me.

I have always told you
How great human beings are.
How great human souls are.
And how great a mission human beings have.

My eternal disciples,
I have taught you before.
The body, face, and mind you now have
May not appear to be emitting a diamond-like brilliance,
But clear your mind and look within you.

Clear your mind and look at your true self.
When you look at your true self with a clear mind,
You will find a diamond-like self there.
You will find the light of a diamond there.
That must have been what I taught you.

Devotion to the Three Treasures

My eternal disciples,
All of you, my disciples,
Hear my voice.

I must have taught you before:
Devote yourself to the Three Treasures.
The Three Treasures are
The Buddha, Dharma, and Sangha.
The Buddha means the Buddha incarnate.
He is the Enlightened One, the Awakened One.
The Dharma is the Laws that the Buddha teaches,
The teachings that the Buddha gives.

The teachings of the Buddha are One Vehicle,
Penetrating through the past, present, and future.
They are one vehicle, one way of teaching,
And one content.
For the past millions of years,
Tens of millions of years,
Or even longer,
Human beings have created various societies,
Various ages,
And various cultures.
Despite having different hues
In each age,
In each region,
And in each culture,
Buddha's Laws have always been One Vehicle.
It means,
The real teachings of the Buddha have existed
Through all ages.

Many of you who hear my voice now
Have probably listened to my teachings in many ways
In the course of your lives

Throughout numerous reincarnations.

These teachings must have always taught one thing.

In the great universe is the Grand Spirit who governs it.

When this Grand Spirit sends a part of Himself to earth,

It becomes the Buddha incarnate.

Because of His mission and authority,

The Buddha incarnate teaches

The Laws of the great Grand Spirit.

The Laws of the great Grand Spirit are taught

Through the Buddha,

And the Laws taught through the Buddha

Will be compiled as scriptures

By the effort of His disciples.

The teachings flowing in these scriptures

Are called the Everlasting Laws.

People must live by these Laws and under these Laws.

It does not matter

Whether the Buddha incarnate is alive on earth;

Even after the Buddha has left the earth,

These Everlasting Laws shall be the Light

To lead many people.

They shall be the beacon of the lighthouse

That will guide many people.

O people,
Blessed are those who were born
When the Buddha is on earth.
Those of you who were born in a time
When the Buddha is not on earth,
Rely on the Laws.
Live by the Laws.
Live under the Laws, and live for the Laws.
It is the Sangha
That nurtures, protects, and spreads Buddha's Laws.
In other words,
The Sangha is the group of the disciples.
How far and wide Buddha's Laws will spread or not
Will depend on the power of this Sangha.

Everlasting Value

My eternal disciples,
Do not compromise with
The value judgment of this age
In which you are now living in this lifetime.
In this current earthly life,

There must be many attractive professions.
There must be many glamorous jobs in a worldly sense.
However, you must not allow your minds
To be caught up in such things.
You must not allow your minds
To be distracted by people's gossip.
You must not allow your minds
To be swayed by people's words.
Throughout your eternal reincarnations,
You have always listened to my words
And followed my words.
Your true, sincere heart
That lies in the depths of your mind
Must surely know what the everlasting value is.
The everlasting value means
Becoming connected to the Laws the Buddha teaches,
Living under the Laws the Buddha teaches,
Promoting and spreading the Laws the Buddha teaches,
Conveying the Laws the Buddha teaches
To each and everyone's heart,
And pouring these Laws into each and everyone's heart
As warm blood.

I am sure you have always believed
These to be the most valuable.

All of you,
Never be deluded by worldly values.
All of you,
Never be deluded by worldly value judgment.
All of you,
Think about the true meaning of your lives.
I must have always taught you
That human beings have eternal lives.
What is most important in living the eternal life
Is to become aware of the great power
That guarantees people an eternal life,
Give gratitude to the great power,
And be determined to live for that great power.
This being so,
Within this great Wheel of Truth,
Let your reincarnations go through its cycles,
Let your life go through its cycles.
The Buddha, Dharma, and Sangha are
Individually precious.

Independent though they may appear,
They are a Trinity.
Even if the Buddha is there,
There is no meaning for the Buddha to incarnate
Without any means to convey the Laws.
Even if the Dharma is there,
It is dead without the Sangha to spread it.
Even if the Sangha is there,
Their hearts have nowhere to rest without the Buddha.
So the Buddha, Dharma, and Sangha bring up each other,
And together, they form a single power.
Truly.
When you think about what the Laws are,
You will know that the Laws are inseparable
From human life.

The Origin of the Soul

All of you, my disciples,
Be aware of how your souls came into being.
Remember how your souls came into being.
Think about the origin of the soul.

You must have already heard:
The Grand Spirit of the great universe
Personified Himself and made His appearance
To place the universe in prosperity and development.
Then, on this Earth too,
There appeared the personified Grand Spirit
Possessing great power.
This personified Grand Spirit used His power
To create a great number of souls.

Yes, this Soul whom you call the Buddha
Is the Parent of your souls.
He created you in great numbers,
Brought you up, and let you learn as your Parent.
This means
The Buddha and the Sangha are like parent and child.
And the Dharma the Buddha teaches is like
The umbilical cord connecting the parent and child—
Mother and her child.
At times, the Dharma is the source supplying nutrition.
At times, the Dharma is the source supplying blood.
At times, the Dharma is the source supplying oxygen.
At times, the Dharma is the source supplying life.

O people,
Know that the Master and disciple
Are like father and child or mother and child.
Know that the Laws are what connect
The parent and child.
As long as you are connected to your Parent
Through the Laws,
You shall never feel hunger or thirst.
You get hungry or thirsty
Because you do not strive to study the Laws,
You do not strive to practice the Laws,
You do not strive to assimilate the Laws as your own.

Renouncing the World

O people,
From now on,
Study well the Laws I teach.
Listen carefully to the words I speak.
I taught you over and over again in the past.
When I descended to earth in a physical body,
I was born into a baby's body.

I grew into a child, then into an adult,

Just like you all.

Eventually,

As I saw various sufferings and anxieties of this world,

I could hardly let them be,

And I renounced the world.

As a renunciant, I intently sought the Path to save people.

In many places,

I broadened my experience and knowledge.

In many places, I meditated.

In many places, I refined my mind.

At times, I learned from people.

At times, I learned from animals.

I learned from

How deer were living, how snakes were living,

How rabbits were living, and how elephants were living.

I also learned how fish in the river were living,

How trees here and there were living,

How flowers in the mountains and the fields were living,

And how the grass was living.

I also learned how honeybees were living

And how butterflies were living.

I learned from all things in this world as my teachers.

To master the true Laws of the Buddha,
I learned and learned,
Refined my mind again and again,
And continued to discipline myself.
And as a result of my six years of spiritual training,
I attained enlightenment.

My Enlightenment

What was the enlightenment I attained?
What is a human being?
What is the mission of human beings?
Why does the universe exist?
And why does the Buddha exist?
What is the relationship between
The Buddha and human beings?
What is the mission,
The purpose of life,
And the happiness of human beings?
What lies behind happiness?
And is it really worth pursuing throughout your life?
I kept on seeking these things over and over

And found the answer.
That was my enlightenment as the Buddha.

Today, many of you may be able to read
About my enlightenment
In various Buddhist scriptures.
However, in the written text,
There is form but no fragrance,
There is shape but no substance.
Are you able to understand my enlightenment?
Are you able to recall my enlightenment—
Recall what you learned in the past?
Can you truly recall even now
The content of my enlightenment
That I had learned and taught?

The Kingdom of the Mind

All of you, my disciples,
I taught you in the past:
No matter how soiled the body you dwell in,
No matter how filthy the clothes you wear,

Even if your body becomes skin and bones,
Your soul has an eternal kingdom within.
The soul, who is the master of this kingdom,
Will become the true king
Only when it manages to control itself,
Its motions, and its lively moves.
You and you alone
Are entitled to become the king of your mind.
No one else but you are entitled to this.

Recall clearly what I taught you.
I taught that you must become the ruler of your mind.
I taught that you must govern
The kingdom of your mind.
The mind becomes freer than ever
As you acquire more power to control it;
Like the Pegasus,
It can freely soar up into the sky
Or gallop across the fields of the earth.
I taught you like this.
First, you must remember these teachings,
Your conviction in these Laws.
It is you who rule over your own mind.

The fact that the mind has been given to you
Means that it is you and only you
Who can fully govern that mind.
There is no such mind that cannot be fully controlled
By your effort
Or through your spiritual training.

I taught you these things in the past,
And I also taught you this:
As you train your mind,
You will find the bud of great mental strength growing.
This very mental strength that you have acquired
Through training your mind
Is the great fruit of your soul training on earth.
You are undergoing spiritual training in this lifetime
To acquire this great mental strength.

Just as your muscles can be trained to exert strong power,
Your mind can be trained and forged
To exert powerful mental strength.
Once you have acquired mental strength in this way,
You cannot conceal it anymore.
It will not weaken.

Its value will not diminish.
That strength is an imperishable treasure to you.
I taught you like this.
I also taught you
That the more you train your minds,
The more powerful your mental strength will be.
As an expedient way to develop your mental strength,
I taught you several ways of spiritual training.
Yes, I gave you some goals of spiritual training.
And the biggest of them
Was surely to abandon your attachment.

For a Higher Purpose

All of you, my disciples,
Can you recall my teachings
Of abandoning attachment?
Can you recall what I described as attachments?
On this earth,
People's will is apt to become weak,
And they tend to be enslaved to their physical bodies.
They will give in to the desires of their bodies

Or the desires that arise from their bodies.
I taught that human beings have such a tendency.
I wouldn't say desires themselves are evil
Because human beings are also creatures
Living under the law of preservation of species.
However, the preservation of species
Must not be for the sake of mere preservation,
As it is for animals and plants.
You, who have studied the Laws,
You, who are undergoing spiritual training
And are called Buddha's disciples,
Must go beyond simple preservation.
You must not make it your goal
Just to live on earth.
Your life on earth is approved
Only when you live for a purpose
That surpasses mere living.
So you must not mistake the *means* to live for the *purpose*.
Your life on earth is a means to support
Something higher.
Your life on earth itself is to serve a higher purpose.
Do not forget that.

It is natural for you to have desires.
These desires themselves are inseparable
From your life's energy.
Abandoning all desires may mean
Cutting off life's energy.
That is why I have always taught you:
Abandon indecent desires,
And abandon vicious thoughts.
I surely told you so.
Abandon sensual lust,
Abandon vicious desires for money,
Abandon vicious desires for dominance,
Abandon vicious desires for possession,
And abandon vicious tendency for gluttony.
I said this to you.
Do not speak obscene words.
Do not act on vicious thoughts.
These things are what I have constantly taught.

The Exploration of Right Mind

All of you, my disciples,
Do you realize
How this teaching of mine is expressed now?

In this lifetime,
I have upheld the exploration of Right Mind.
This is exactly the same teaching I gave in the past
When I told you to get rid of your vicious desires,
Obscene thoughts, and evil emotions.
This is another aspect of
The exploration of what is right.
You must enter the Right Path.
You must explore the Right Path.
To explore the Right Path,
You must control the emotions, thoughts, and deeds
That arise from living as human beings.
You must control the thoughts that pop up
In your minds.
You must control the motives behind your actions.
If your actions indicate being evil,
It means you need to practice self-reflection.

I surely taught you
The principle of forgiveness as well.
As long as you are human beings,
You will sometimes have wrong thoughts.
Because you are human beings,
You will sometimes do wrong deeds.
As long as you are deluded human beings on earth,
Far from being perfect or flawless,
You will have to face temptations
And live through them many times.
However, do not bemoan or lament
Having to live through those sufferings.
Even if you are in a state of suffering,
You have been given a way
To wipe your evil clean and purify your mind
Through the practice of self-reflection.
That is the Eightfold Path
I have always taught you.
So take it seriously.

Like a Lotus Flower

All of you, my disciples,
I loved lotus flowers.
I often talked about parables using lotus flowers.
Look at the muddy waters there.
Look at the muddy waters here.
The waters where lotus flowers bloom
Are all unsightly.
No, to put it another way,
They are filthy waters.
They are by no means clean.
The waters are muddy, sometimes giving off a foul scent.
Such muddy waters are chosen
For lotus seeds to be sown,
And in such muddy waters, lotus flowers dare to bloom.
They stretch their untainted stems
Above the muddy waters
And bloom as exceptionally beautiful pink flowers,
Purple flowers, and white flowers.
Indeed, they seem to be out of this world.

All of you, my disciples,
Be aware that your mission also lies here.
Know that your calling also lies here.
This world on earth may appear to be full of dirt.
This world may be filled with temptations.
This world may always be filled with the risks of falling.
However, you must not avoid such an environment.
You must not try to escape from such an environment.
Even in such muddy waters
Bloom beautiful lotus flowers.
That is the meaning of you being born
In this lifetime as my disciples.
I taught you like this before,
And now I shall teach you again.
No matter how unhappy this world may be,
No matter how difficult this world may be,
Do not make it an excuse.

The Salvation of All Humankind

If you believe my voice,
Believe also my words here:

When Buddha and His disciples are born into this world,
It is always an age covered in dark clouds.
It is when people's minds have been devastated
And when the times are about to plunge into
The lowest of the lows.
There is a meaning for Buddha's disciples
To be born into such an age.
That is exactly when
Saving all humankind becomes possible.
No matter what age you are born in,
No matter what environment you are born in,
No matter what kinds of people you are born among,
You must not regret it.
The age you descend to,
The age you are born in,
Is always a time of suffering
And a time of sadness for humankind.
But your mission must be
To declare the dawn of a new age
In this age of darkness.
Only then can you fulfill your promise to Buddha.

Come, Follow Me

All of you, my disciples,
I am happy I could see you again in this lifetime.
I am happy I could see you again in this lifetime.
I promised you in the past:
I would come back in the Final Days of the Laws.
I would be reborn again in the Final Days of the Laws
To devote my life to creating Buddha Land
Together with you.
I would rather descend to this world
In the Final Days of the Laws
To teach the new Laws.
I promised you this in the past.
I have never broken this promise.
Now that the Final Days of the Laws have come,
The age is calling for me,
And the age is calling for you.

My eternal disciples,
Believe my voice.
Awaken to my voice.
Follow my lead.

Come, follow me.
Come, follow my White Hand.
I am your Eternal Master.
It is the mission of the disciples
To follow your Eternal Master.
Never, ever forget this.

CHAPTER TWO

Words of Wisdom

All of you, my disciples,
Listen to my words carefully.
I have taught you again and again that
You must always have a guide for the mind.
Your mind constantly wavers left and right,
But you must always have a guide for the mind,
As if heading toward the North Star.
I have always taught you this.

Nourishment for the Mind

This guide for the mind means
Words of wisdom.
You must learn many words of wisdom
And make them food for your minds as you live.
O people,
The words of wisdom cannot be found everywhere.
The words of wisdom are given to you
When you need them, and in an appropriate way,
During the course of your life.
Today, my words are also recorded and read
In great numbers

As the words of wisdom.
But the time when these words were spoken,
The place these words were spoken,
And the people to whom these words were spoken
Are not necessarily clear.
So, many of the readers will not know
Whom these words were spoken to,
In which place, in which way, or in which time period.
In fact, words are very delicate;
Unless they are said in the right place,
To the right people, and at the right time,
They can hardly gain true power.

All of you, my disciples,
The words I speak and the lectures I give
Will be understood differently
Depending on the state of your minds
And the time you hear or read them.
Therefore,
All of you, my disciples,
Do not interpret my words
Only in your own ways.
Try to explore the true meaning of my words.

My words do not necessarily answer
Your personal problems.
My words are spoken for many people.
From among the words I have spoken to many people,
Choose the ones that nourish your minds.
Find the ones that resonate in your minds.
Pick out the words that naturally come to you,
That you think are universal.
Those are the words of wisdom.

The Words of Self-Discipline

O people,
When things are going well,
Human beings are apt to become conceited.
To prevent yourself from becoming
Conceited in favorable times,
You need the words of self-discipline.
It is important to make efforts to discipline yourself.
You need to constantly engrave into your heart
The words of self-discipline,
Keep telling them to yourself,

And keep picturing them in your head.
What are the words of self-discipline?
They are the words to remind you of the fact:
At the height of success,
People are apt to forget that
They will inevitably become overconfident.

All of you, my disciples,
Do not be overconfident with your ability.
Even if you have made a great achievement
As a result of your taking action,
Do not be overconfident.
Do not overvalue that.
Do not take credit for it.

You are connected to the Eternal Life.
You are connected to the Energy of the great Grand Spirit.
You are one with the Energy of Buddha,
And you are part of the Energy of Buddha.
That is why, when you believe in Buddha
And practice His Laws,
You will surely make many great achievements.
You will surely accomplish many great things.

You will surely witness many great miracles.
However,
Do not think that they came from your own power.
Do not think that you have done them by yourself.
These miracles occurred
Only because your life is connected
To the Great Energy of the universe.
You were able to accomplish them
Only because you are one with the Great Wisdom.

All of you,
You must know that
There is nothing in this universe
That you can accomplish by yourself alone.
You must know that
You are on the Palm of the great Buddha.
This very existence of Buddha's Palm
Allows you to walk on His Palm.
When Buddha closes His Palm,
The universe will become pitch black.
When Buddha opens His Palm,
The universe will be filled with infinite light.
You must not forget

That you are living on the Palm of Buddha.
Nothing can be achieved with your power alone.
What you believe you have accomplished
Was accomplished by dint of Buddha's power.
Do not forget this attitude.
You need to constantly engrave in your minds
This great secret of the universe.

The Middle Way

I tell you again and again.
In times of success,
People climb up the ladders of success,
But at the same time,
They are also climbing down to failure.
Do not forget this.
The road to success and the road to failure
Are two sides of the same coin;
This becomes clearer and more evident
As their slopes become steeper.
People who never succeed
Seldom experience failure.

But those who have many successes
Will also experience many failures.
Life is like a twisted strand of rope,
Constantly showing the right or the left strand,
Or the upper or the lower strand.
Likewise,
Happiness and unhappiness are
The upper and the lower strands of the same rope.
Do not forget this.

You have probably shaken a rope to make waves before.
When a wave is created,
Its crest and trough are not completely different things.
The same part of the rope forms a crest at one moment
And a trough the next to hit the ground.
In the same way,
Your life can be at a crest or a trough
Depending on the time.
However, I say to you:
At any time,
Be true to your hearts,
And always keep the Middle Way.

The principle of the Middle Way is by no means
A principle to keep you from success
Or save you from the depths of failure only.
The principle of the Middle Way
Is the royal road of life.
Know that here lies the royal road of life.
In other words,
In times of success,
When things are going well for you,
Or when you are on the rising tide of opportunity,
Constantly discipline yourself and live humbly.
Be humble and, at the same time,
Always be thankful for others and for Buddha.
If you remember to be humble and grateful
During successful and favorable times,
Your success will continue to grow.
No matter how great your success may become,
You are still on the Middle Way.
Success that stays on the Middle Way
Is accompanied by humility and gratitude.
Success accompanied by humility and gratitude
Is always on the Middle Way

Because it is the path that brings up all people.
Your becoming successful must not invite
Others' failures.
Your success must not harm others.
Your success must not make others unhappy.
The path to success
Must be the way to nurture all people.

The way to nurture everyone is a great road.
It is a wide road.
It is a flat road.
It is a road that takes you infinitely far.
Such a road is the Middle Way.
The Middle Way is also the Golden Road.
The road that emits a golden light—
That is the Middle Way.
All of you,
You must know this well.

What Makes Your Soul Shine

Even so, all of you,
You must not lament even when you are unhappy.
It is in these times of unhappiness
That you deserve to enter the Middle Way.
In times of unhappiness,
Many of you are probably regretting your lives.
You have probably examined your mistakes thoroughly
And deeply felt how shameful you are.
At such times,
You are preparing yourself to enter the Golden Road.
From despair
You must rise again
Because you, too,
Are the hands and legs of Buddha,
Because you, too,
Are part of the Great Energy of Buddha.
If you are such beings,
There is no such thing as failure in this world.
There is no such thing as a setback in this world.
There is no such thing as
Being plunged into unhappiness
Or into the depths of misery.

What appear to be failures, setbacks, or misfortunes
Are all there to make your souls shine.
They are whetstones to make your souls shine.
You must understand them like this.
This is the basis of Buddha's Laws.
I will not say
There are no sufferings or difficulties in this world.
I will not say
There are no sufferings or difficulties in another world.
But these sufferings and difficulties do not exist
As something good in and of themselves.
They are not allowed to exist simply for what they are.
I believe so.

Sufferings and difficulties are allowed to exist
Only to serve as whetstones.
Sufferings and difficulties are the whetstones
To polish your souls and make them shine.
Indeed, they are the sandpaper to file your souls.
O people,
Understand sufferings and difficulties in this way.
This being so,
If you are in the midst of suffering,
Know what destiny is trying to teach you.

Know the lessons destiny is trying to give you,
And make them nourishment for your minds.
Make them your personal commandments.
Turn your failures into lessons,
And return to the Middle Way.
As you walk on the Middle Way,
You may again be hit by the same pattern of danger.
At that time,
Use the knowledge, experience,
And wisdom you have acquired.
Then, you shall not repeat the same mistakes.
That is because what you have experienced,
What you have learned from these experiences,
Or the lessons you have gained through these experiences
And the wisdom born of them
Will protect you,
Adorning your foreheads with Light.

Therefore, do not fear failure.
Understand failure as a vaccine given by Buddha
For you to achieve yet a greater success
And protect you from yet a greater failure in the future.
Understand that it is a vaccine given by Buddha.
It was given to you to train your souls

And to fill your lives with much Light.
When you enter the Middle Way in this way,
You are promised to be blessed with Eternal Light.

Humility and Gratitude

All of you, my disciples,
I have always taught you this as well.
Again and again, I taught you that
You should not pursue happiness only for yourself,
And it is not enough for you alone to be happy.
Know that
When you enter the Middle Way and become happy,
This happiness is not only yours.
You must return
The happiness you found on the Middle Way
To many people around you,
Making it the power to save the people around you.
I believe so.

Why does the Middle Way exist?
Have you ever really pondered this?

Suppose you have strayed from the Middle Way
And are walking on a thorny path of suffering.
At that time,
People must be desperate to save you somehow.
They must be absorbed in how to save you.
The fact that
You are causing many people to worry and suffer
Shows that you are now living a negative life.
That is why you must quickly leave this thorny path
And return to the Middle Way.

I taught you to be humble and grateful
When things are going well for you.
Do you understand what I mean?
What does it mean to be humble?
It means to remind yourself
That you are receiving help from many people
And that you are receiving the power of Buddha.
To be humble means to constantly tell this to yourself
And prevent yourself from becoming conceited.

Then what is gratitude?
It is the action born of being humble.

Because you are humble, you can be grateful.
When you feel grateful,
Your humility will manifest
As good deeds to others.
This is very important.
Successful people are allowed to be as such
Because they are giving love to many other people.
Yes, those who have great harvests in their fields
May often be envied or slandered by others.
But there is a way for you to make others happy
Even by having great harvests in your fields.
That is to go out and give away a great amount of fruit,
Rice, and wheat that you have harvested
To the people around you.
Then, you will become love incarnate.
Then, your very existence will become goodness itself.
You will become goodness incarnate.
Truly.
Here lies the very essence of success.
When you try to use the fruits of your success
Only for yourself,
You will make a great mistake.
But when you try to use the fruits of your success
For the sake of many people,

You will be able to enrich the world
And bring joy to the souls of many people.

The Practice of Love

All of you, my disciples,
I tell you:
Successful people are like a canal
Running through the fields.
The canal runs straight across the fields.
It runs straight, carrying plentiful, clean water.
The canal provides water
To all the fields in the area.
Know that this is the way of successful people.
No matter how much water you keep,
It will never turn into virtue.
No matter how much water you keep,
It will never turn into goodness.
No matter how much water you keep,
It will never turn into success.
However,
When you release that water into the canal
And let it flow, irrigating the vast fields,

It will become your virtue,
Your goodness,
And your success.

O people,
When you think of the Middle Way,
Imagine how this canal is.
If the canal only runs along
The perimeter of the vast fields,
The water will not be able to irrigate them all.
Only when the canal runs through
The middle of the fields
Will it be able to supply others with plentiful love.
The canal always runs through the middle,
And it is always at the center of the fields.
The fields develop around the canal,
And the canal runs to develop the fields.
In a sense, water is like blood,
While canals are like blood vessels circulating the blood.
And the heart that pumps this blood through the vessels
Is your heart of love.
Do not forget this.
Make it the ideal of your life to become like this canal.

You must become like the great pump
That provides water into the canal.
You must be like this pump
That continually draws up groundwater
And keeps on supplying water to the canal
When the fields are in need of water.
The groundwater that wells up boundlessly
Is actually Buddha's Light.
It is Buddha's Mercy.
You must know
The way to receive Buddha's Love
With your whole bodies.
When you generously try to fill others with love,
When you try to quench the thirst
Of other people's hearts,
Buddha's Power, Love, Courage, and Light will well up
Just like the groundwater.
You must never doubt this.
I tell you again and again.
Here lies the ideal of life.
This is where the ideal of life must be.

The Way to Cultivate Yourself

I add yet the following point.
Let me elaborate on and expand
This analogy of the canal.
Each canal has a certain width,
Which may vary from that of other canals;
Some are one foot wide,
While others are two feet or three feet wide.
They need a certain width, a certain length, and barriers
To let the water flow.
At a glance,
This may seem to be blocking the love for others.
People may criticize and denounce you
For having such barriers.
But think about it.
What will happen
If the canals do not run straight as they are supposed to?
What will happen
If water simply gushes out of the pump house?
The surrounding areas will be drenched in water,
Creating a small flood.
As a result of this flooding,

Will the rice seedlings truly grow?
Think about it,
And you know they will not.
Those seedlings that are yet to fully grow
May drown in the pools of water and rot away.
I think so.

So this analogy of the canal tells you
That you need to construct the foundation of life
To give love to more people far and wide.
You may have doubts when you are digging a canal.
You may be criticized by others
During the process of building a canal.
Their criticisms will mostly be like this:
"If you have enough land
To build a two or three feet wide canal,
You could have a greater harvest
By planting rice and wheat there."
Many people may well say so.
However, you shall keep on digging a canal in silence.
Some people may mock you
As they watch you continue to dig,
Compact the soil, and work to run water.

"You are a fool.
Even if you build a canal,
You wouldn't get a single grain of rice or wheat
From that land.
You are wasting your time on meaningless work.
You are working on it for mere self-satisfaction."
There will always be people who criticize you like this.

However, never doubt your ideal.
Never let go of your ideal.
No matter how grand your plan may be,
It will definitely be achieved one day.
Do not be caught up in the immediate future.
Do not be caught up in the immediate gain.
Do not be daunted by the criticism or slander of others
When you are pursuing a grand ideal.
Just focus on digging a canal straight,
Without feeling daunted by such criticism or slander.
Even if you are told that the land will be wasted,
Even if you are told that
Your work will not produce even a single grain of wheat,
Even if you are told that it is a waste of effort,
You must not stop building a canal

If you make it your life's ideal to supply great love.
I believe so.
When you think like this,
You will see that keeping the Middle Way
Is not such an easy thing for you.
Once the canal is finished, successful, and complete,
Others will finally understand
And be convinced of its effect.
But before completion,
You may see a lot of people saying, "What's the point?"
You may hear a lot of people saying, "What's the point?"
These are the words of those
Who cannot understand your ideal.

All of you, my disciples,
Do you understand what I am trying to say
Using this parable of the canal?
Do you understand the meaning of this parable?

My eternal disciples,
I am saying that
There is so much to learn
To walk the way to human perfection.

You must cultivate yourselves.
You must walk the path of cultivating yourselves.
Cultivating yourself is not an easy task.
It requires continuous, diligent efforts.
When you are cultivating yourselves,
You may at times be criticized by many people.
"There is no point in studying."
"You are studying for nothing."
There will surely be times
When you are told like this.
However, the way to cultivate yourselves
Is a long, grand path.
It is a way to nourish your souls
And a way to bring up your souls.
Tell yourselves
That you are now trying to build a canal
In the vast land.
With this single canal,
You can water the arid lands around you
And turn them into bountiful fields.
Building this canal is equal to cultivating yourself.

For you to triumph in life and guide many people,
I believe you must gain by all means

A great deal of knowledge,
Accumulate a great deal of experiences,
And raise them to the level of culture.
I do not call those who amass some pieces of knowledge
As cultured people.
It is true that knowledge will become the power
To cultivate yourselves.
But it is through love that knowledge becomes culture.
Knowledge will become culture for the first time
Through the catalyst of love.
I want to tell you so.
What matters is
The purpose of your acquiring knowledge.
If you are acquiring knowledge
Only to make yourselves look good
And to make others feel how great you are,
Then that knowledge will never become your culture.
However, if you are acquiring knowledge
To benefit and nurture other people,
That knowledge will be absorbed
Deep into your characters,
Enriching and empowering your characters.
So the way to cultivate yourself
Becomes the way of a cultured person itself

When love is added to your knowledge as a catalyst
And your knowledge turns into your own wisdom.

O people,
Never doubt this.
Listen, from now on,
Keep a part of the vast land stretching before you
To cultivate yourselves.
By this, I am saying that you must keep
A part of your life's time that lies ahead of you
To cultivate yourselves.
Set aside a certain amount of time each day,
A certain amount of time each month,
And a certain amount of time each year
For you to cultivate yourselves.
This time will never be wasted.
It will become the groundwork
To nurture many people.
This is what I am saying.

Then, what is the best way to cultivate yourselves?
The best of all culture, or the true culture,
Is, of course, the eternal Buddha's Truth.

I believe so.
Place Buddha's Truth at the center of your culture.
Learn based on Buddha's Truth.
Place Buddha's teachings
At the core of your culture.
And after knowing and learning them,
Re-learn the knowledge
That exists in this world in large amounts.
Re-study it all.
And re-examine the experiences you had in the past.
Pick out the diamond-like brilliance
From the many experiences you had in the past.
If you find a piece of wisdom
In what you studied in the past,
Pick it up and adorn yourselves with it.
If, in your current studies,
You find something that hints at Buddha's Truth
Or that you think carries Buddha's Truth,
Absorb it as if you are devouring it.
Study it well.
In other words,
The way to cultivate yourselves
Is to place Buddha's Truth at the center

And add the many legacies of humankind around it,
Which are called inventions, discoveries, and innovations.
A lot of people have made many discoveries,
A lot of people have developed many innovations,
A lot of people have developed many philosophies,
A lot of people have voiced many opinions.
Screen all of them using the sieve called Buddha's Truth,
And assimilate what has passed through the sieve
To nourish yourselves.
This is a wonderful thing to do
To cultivate yourselves.

The Path to Improve Yourself

All of you, my disciples,
Do you understand what I mean?
All of you, my disciples,
You must not feel overwhelmed.
You must not lament over the pain
Of constantly walking the road to improve yourselves,
Of tirelessly walking the road of making efforts.
You must believe that this road is the Golden Road.

Absorb nutrition every day,
And develop your bodies every day.
Absorb spiritual nourishment every day,
Strengthen the foundations of your souls every day,
And make your souls even greater every day.
That is the true meaning of your lives,
The true significance of your lives.

O people, from now on,
Make efforts steadily and tirelessly.
And engrave many lessons into your hearts.
Continuously engraving lessons into your hearts
Is the proof that you have walked the path of discipline.
You may have heard the term "Right Effort"
In the Eightfold Path.
Right Effort is a difficult concept for people today.
But I dare say
The path of Right Effort
Is a path that infinitely refines your characters.
It is a path that infinitely leads you to Buddha.
Never give up on walking this path
That leads to Buddha.
Even if you run out of energy on the way,

You must never think of turning back.
Even if you get stuck
And can no longer move forward,
Do not look back.
Take a rest where you are, stop for a while,
Wait until your strength returns,
And once you are filled with strength,
Start walking this path to improve yourselves.
This is the great mission assigned to you all.
I must say that Buddha's Laws are powerless
If they do not serve to improve people.
For Buddha's Laws to be truly powerful teachings,
Many of those who learn them must gain courage,
Be filled with wisdom,
And walk the path to improve themselves with hope.
You, too, must walk this path to improve yourself—
Yes, in other words, this path to enlightenment.
This is the path
That you are to ultimately aim for.

CHAPTER THREE

Do Not Be Foolish

All of you, my disciples,
Listen to my words carefully.
Listen to my words carefully,
And engrave them into your mind.
Today, I will tell you about fools.
Rather, I will tell you *not* to be fools.

What Is Foolishness?

Look, the world is full of fools everywhere.
Do you understand the difference
Between those who are foolish and those who are not?
To determine who are foolish,
You may try to distinguish the wise from the unwise.
It is true that
This is one of the ways to distinguish the two.
However, I tell you,
Many people in the world believe they are not foolish.
But there are many fools
Among those who believe they are not.
Whether you are smart or not,
That alone does not determine

Whether you are foolish or not.
Whether or not you are a fool depends on
Whether or not you are aware of what your soul wants.
Now, take a look around.
There must be fools around you as well.
In fact, you, yourself, may be the one living foolishly.
Being foolish means
Living while making poison in your mind,
Living while taking poison in your mind,
And living without realizing
You are actually swallowing poison.
If you take in poisonous food,
Your body will immediately wither,
Eventually leading you to your deathbed.
Your soul may be taking in toxins now,
So why are you not aware
That they will lead to the death of your soul?
Why are you not aware of it?

All of you, listen to me carefully.
Every day, you take in toxins without realizing it.
Every day, you take in arsenic.
Even if it is a small amount of toxin,

If you take it every day,
It will gradually accumulate in you to a large amount
And will eventually drive your souls to death.
What is the death of a soul?
It means
The soul no longer possesses the Buddha-nature
That it should.
What does it mean
For a soul to no longer possess the Buddha-nature
That it should?
It means
The soul will allow itself to live against
The original purpose of why it was created.

Do Not Be Greedy

All of you, listen carefully.
I will tell you.
First, abandon your greed.
Many of you probably have a greedy mind.
Do you understand what a greedy mind is?
It is a mind that constantly seeks to take.

It is a mind that craves this and that.
A greedy mind includes
The desire for position,
The desire for promotion,
And the desire for fame.
When you keep craving something
Like the hungry ghosts
Who are never satisfied no matter how much they eat,
Your souls fall into the infinite depths of murky water.
You must know this.
Do you understand why greed is poison?
Do you know why greed is evil?
Do you know what it means?

A Heart of Offering

All of you, my disciples,
I have taught you again and again.
It is difficult for human beings
To have life and be born into this world.
It is difficult to be born into this world
And encounter the teachings of Buddha.

It is also difficult to be born
Into the same age as Buddha.
It is difficult to be born during the age
When Buddha is alive and is teaching.
Since you were born into such an age,
Your mission shall naturally be clear.
You have come to give to many people.
"To give" is a modern term.
It means to have a heart of offering.
What do I mean by offering?
It is the thoughtful heart toward others.
It is the heart to do good to others.
It is the heart to serve others.
Without such a heart,
Buddha's teachings would be meaningless.
The teachings of Buddha exist to serve others.
The teachings of Buddha exist to offer
Something to others.
The teachings of Buddha exist to give love to others.

All of you,
You must not mistake this fundamental point.
Know that you were not born to be greedy.

If you look into your minds
And find strong greed,
I must say you are foolish.
Stop being attached to your social status.
Stop being attached to your promotion.
Stop being attached to your honor.
Stop being attached to your pride.
Do not be attached to your desire
To look good in the eyes of others.
These desires are all greed.
The desire to look good in others' eyes
And the desire to be highly respected are greed.
The desire to be admired
And the desire to become famous are also greed.
The desire to wield your power is greed as well.

The Enlightened Ones

O people,
The enlightened ones are always calm.
O people,
The enlightened ones walk with meekness.

O people,
The enlightened ones smile as they walk.
O people,
The enlightened ones are not arrogant.
The enlightened ones are not haughty.
The enlightened ones
Never try to make themselves look good.
The enlightened ones do not try to judge others.
The enlightened ones do not try to harm others.
The enlightened ones are meek,
Speak the right words,
And are always serene and graceful.
The poison of greed is so evil
Because it damages your meekness.
Meekness is worthy in and of itself.
Meek facial expression, meek words, and meek manner
Are worthy in and of themselves.
Meekness itself shows how Buddha is.

O people, from now on,
Check carefully and thoroughly
Whether or not you have greed in your mind.
If you find the poison of greed in your mind,

Grab it immediately and throw it away.
Never allow it to enter your mind again.
Close the door and never let it in again.

Know Yourself

There are yet many more fools in the world.
One type of fool is those who do not know themselves,
Who do not know who they are.
They do not know who they really are,
And yet they are proud of themselves.
However, I will say to you repeatedly:
Even if you read tens of thousands of books,
Even if you travel across the whole world,
If you cannot fully understand yourself,
You cannot be called wise.
No matter how much knowledge
You cram into your head,
Even if you become a walking dictionary,
And even if you visit all regions, trek to every place,
And travel across the whole world,
If you do not know your mind

And do not know your true nature,
You cannot be called wise.
On the other hand,
Even if your knowledge is poor
And your experience is limited,
If you know your mind well,
Control your mind well,
And have awakened to your true self,
You are worthy to be called wise.

O people,
Do not mistake the right order.
First, it is important to govern yourselves.
No matter how much money you use,
How many days you spend,
Or how much help you receive from many people
To make great achievements,
If you fail to know yourselves and govern yourselves well,
Then you cannot be called wise.
Know yourselves well.
Knowing yourselves includes
Knowing the fact that you are children of Buddha.
No matter how much you are respected

In this worldly sense,
If you do not know that
Your bodies and souls have been given by Buddha
And live without being aware of
Your Buddha-nature within,
You can never be called wise.

I tell you again and again.
First, you must know yourselves well.
Make this your first goal.
If you do not know yourselves,
No matter how much you may boast
That you have understood the world and other people,
It does not make you wise.
No matter how much knowledge you may accumulate,
If you do not know yourselves,
I must say you are foolish.

The Most Foolish Ones

O people,
There are yet other kinds of fools.

These fools take pleasure
In drawing other people's attention to themselves
And dragging others into worry and confusion.
There are also those
Who poison other people's minds,
Evoke impatience in other people's minds,
Bring other people to the abyss of temptations,
Lie to other people and whisper in their ears,
And try to delude
Those walking on the path of spiritual training.
These people are also fools.
Such fools sometimes appear
From among those who study my teachings.
There are an endless number of people
Who try to drag others onto their boat
Just because they cannot advance in their enlightenment,
Just because they are not given important positions.
They try to shake the firmly determined minds
Of their fellow spiritual practitioners
In an attempt to expand their group.
They try to increase the number of those
Who are discontent and grumbling like they are.

O people, know that
Such a mind, such a thought, and such an action
Will all be connected to hell.
Many lost souls are living in hell.
These lost souls do not try to be saved.
Instead of trying to be saved,
They try to increase the number of their fellows.
They try to drag other people into their group.
They try to alleviate their own sufferings
By making others experience the same sufferings,
By making others have the same delusions,
And by making others fall into the abyss of desires.
However, I tell you:
Continuing to carry out these actions
Will never bring you peace.
That is not what you should do.
To lessen your own sufferings,
Do not try to use other people.
Do not try to drag other people to join your group.
Do not try to complain to other people.
You alone are enough to endure your sufferings.
You alone must confront your sufferings.
Confront your own problems by yourselves.

Do not instead team up with others,
Rushing to justify and rationalize yourselves together.
Never, ever do such a thing.
Indeed, those who follow and learn the Laws
Must not twist or distort the teachings,
Spread the teachings incorrectly,
Or lure others
To justify themselves.
Know that these actions are all connected to hell.

So I will tell you.
One of the most foolish ones of all are those who
Delude people on the path of spiritual discipline.
They do not realize that they are foolish.
They do not think they are foolish.
Rather, they believe they are right and wise.
They then distort and twist even the teachings of Buddha
With their limited intellect
And try to give convenient explanations
For themselves.
However, wise people must know
What kind of sin will be produced by such an attitude.
At the basis of this attitude is a desire.

At the basis of this attitude is the desire to stand
In an equally great position
As the one who preaches the Laws.
However, all of you,
Know this well:
People have their own caliber.
There is a right order in guiding others.
The great souls who achieved great things
In the long process of reincarnation
Are walking ahead of others,
So they are expected to lead others who follow behind.
But those who are still immature
In terms of their behaviors and minds
And are yet to practice enough spiritual training
Must continue to receive guidance.
Know that such a difference in position
Has existed in all ages.
To learn well, you must behave well.
To know well, you must be humble.
To be enlightened well,
You must govern yourselves well.
That is important.

The Value of Kindness

I have more to say about not being foolish.
Foolish people often do not have kindness in their hearts.
They are likely to live without knowing
How important it is to have kindness in their hearts.
Kindness means
To make many people feel happy to be alive.
Some people do not have such kindness,
And instead,
Live by nonchalantly pushing others away,
Making others obey them,
Making others fear and shrink before them,
Or making others kneel at their feet.
These people must be unaware
Of how mistakenly they have been living.
The value of kindness is that it is the greatest proof
To show that human beings are children of Buddha.
To express this kindness,
I sometimes use the word "sadness."
People living on earth,
Or fellow human beings living on earth,
Are in the midst of many sufferings.
Many are living in suffering

Within the bondage of the physical body.
They are living in suffering within the world
Where there are many obstacles to enlightenment
And yet only a few chances to find enlightenment.
The same is true with animals and plants.
You will see many fellow beings
Who are living while suffering
In this world of the third dimension,
In this phenomenal world.
Looking at these fellow beings,
Do you not shed tears?
If you do not,
There is no kindness in your hearts.
Shedding tears at others' sufferings and sadness
Is called "Great Compassion."
It is called "Great Sorrow."
These are also the tears of Buddha's mercy and love.
True kindness will lead to true sadness.
When you look at the world full of sadness
And see thorns stuck in people's bodies,
Why not think of removing those thorns for them?
If a poisoned pin is stuck in people's hearts,
Why not try to remove it for them?

O people,
When people have lost the feeling of sadness,
They become self-centered.
They think only of themselves.
They think only of their own happiness.
That is how human beings are.
Look at the world,
Look at people,
Look at animals,
Look at plants,
And feel the sadness in them.
This sadness shall teach you
What you must do now.

The Folly of Self-Preservation

Those who do not know sadness
Will think only about themselves.
They will think about their own sadness.
However,
No matter how much they think about
Their own sadness,

This will never make the world better.
In order to create a better world,
Remove the thorns stuck in other people's hearts.
Remove the poisoned pin stuck in other people's hearts.
You must have such an attitude.
You must never try to hurt others.
You must never try to harm others.
Never have such an attitude.
Self-preservation that only tries to benefit yourself
Is another characteristic of foolish people.
They are working tirelessly
To distinguish themselves, and only themselves,
But the direction of their efforts
Is far from the Will of Buddha.
Can't they see
That by trying to distinguish themselves only,
They are even ruining themselves?
Can't they see
That they were not given life in this lifetime
Only to think of themselves?
The fact that you have been given life in this lifetime
Means that you must not use your lives
Only for yourselves.

You have been blessed with extraordinary mercy
To be given life in this lifetime.
This means that
With gratitude for such blessings,
You have to enrich the hearts of many people.
You must know that.
That is why,
Do not think too much about yourself only.
Do not think too much of your happiness only.
Your desire to benefit yourself
Must by no means bring harm to others.
I surely taught you in the past:
Your desire to benefit yourself
Must not lead to harm others
While only benefitting yourself.
Your desire to benefit yourself is allowed
Only when benefitting yourself benefits others.
You must have good control over yourself,
Have good control over your mind,
Polish your soul,
And enter the wonderful world.
If, by polishing yourself,
You managed to improve others,

Improve the world,
And make this world—Buddha's creation—
A beautiful place,
Then you must be content with that.
Do not misunderstand this point.

Do Not Be Troubled by Your Physical Body

Furthermore, I say to you:
You are still far from knowing
That you are foolish.
Many of you get overly caught up
In your physical appearances.
Many of you get overly caught up
In the concerns about your physical bodies.
Looking at your physical bodies,
You probably agonize and fret over the fact
That you are too tall or too short,
Too fat or too thin,
Or attractive or unattractive.
And you probably talk about it every day.

However, I believe these are also
The thoughts of foolish people.
Physical bodies are just vehicles.
They are the boats,
So if they serve for souls
To carry out spiritual training in this lifetime,
That is fine.
Do not expect more than that.
If your body sufficiently serves for your soul training,
Isn't it enough?
You must not ask for more than that.
You must not bother your mind
About anything more.
It is important that
You swear to your heart
That you will not be overly troubled
By your physical body
Or because of your physical body.
There are other things you should worry about.
It is about your mind.
It is your mind that you must worry about.
Worry that your mind is bad,
That your mind is full of mistakes.

Worry whether your mind is beautiful or not.
If your mind is not beautiful,
It will naturally show.
If your mind is not beautiful,
Your eyes will not be beautiful either.
If your mind is disturbed,
If your mind is impure,
Your eyes will become clouded.
Your eyes will have an evil glow.
Your eyes will reflect wicked feelings.
If your mind is arrogant,
Your nose will seem to stick up more than it really does.
It will always appear to be pointing straight up.
If your mind is not righteous,
Your mouth will appear crooked.
If you are constantly sarcastic and critical of others,
Your mouth will point this out and be crooked.
It will show your ugliness.
If your mind is not calm,
It will show in your bearings.
If you are constantly blaming and abusing others,
Such qualities will be reflected in your bearings.

However, those with a peaceful mind
Will make others unconscious of time
While living in the flow of time,
Unconscious of the region
While living in the region,
And unconscious of the people around them
While being among them.
That is because they are always meek and calm.
The physical body of a person
Whose mind is meek and calm
Never makes people around them feel unpleasant.
O people,
Before taking care of your physical bodies,
First, take care of your minds.
Before trying to make your physical bodies beautiful,
First, make your minds beautiful.
Every day, be meek.
Do not be angry.
Do not slander others.
Do not complain.
Deeply engrave these points into your minds.

Do Not Be Angry

All of you, my disciples,
I just listed several poisons of the mind.
You must not be angry.
Come what may,
No matter how much you are humiliated,
You must not get angry.
"Do not be angry"
Is an extremely important teaching
For those who practice spiritual training.
As you practice spiritual training,
You may sometimes be criticized by others,
Condemned, or humiliated.
However,
If you are disciples of Buddha,
Endure such humiliations.
You must not respond to anger with anger.
To anger, respond with calm words.
To harsh criticisms, respond with silence.
Do not forget to smile.
Do not forget to have a mind of perseverance.
Do not forget to have a mind of endurance.

This mind of endurance,
This discipline of perseverance,
Will serve to accumulate virtue in you.
Know that there is no virtue
In those who do not have the mind of endurance.
Know that you can never become a virtuous person
As long as you are responding to anger with anger.
You must never, ever be angry.

Do Not Envy

Also, you must not be jealous or envious.
This is another point you must keep in mind.
You must never become jealous or envious of others.
This is also an important teaching
For those who practice spiritual training.
As you practice spiritual training,
You may hear of the good reputation of someone else
Or of someone advancing in their state of mind,
And before you know it,
You may start feeling envious or jealous of them.
However, you must not give in to these feelings.

You must know that
Accumulating jealousy and envy in your mind
Is a foolish way to live.
You must not have such a mind.
If you meet great people,
Love them,
Admire them,
And respect them.
By respecting great people,
You can get closer to them for the first time.
By respecting great people,
You, too, are firmly taking the first step to progress.
No poison is more terrifying than that of envy
For those who practice spiritual training.
Because of this poison of envy,
Ten or twenty years of your spiritual training
Will disappear instantly, like bubbles.
By harboring envy,
The virtue you have strived so hard to accumulate so far
Will disappear instantly.
Envy is not good
Because it does not make anyone happy.
It does not bring happiness to those who are envied,

Nor does it to you, yourself, who are envious.
Envy disturbs the harmony of mind and peace of mind.
Once you know that envy is evil,
Never be envious.
Admire and love great people.
Love those with talent, love those with experience,
And love those with wisdom.
This is important.

Without the heart of loving those with talent,
Those with experience, and those with wisdom,
You cannot respect the Three Treasures, either.
You cannot love your Master, your Master's teachings,
And the group Master created, either.
Then, your soul training in this lifetime
Will become very difficult.

Do Not Complain

I told you that you must not be angry.
I also taught you that you must not be envious.
And yes,

The next thing you must keep yourself away from
Is complaining.
Complaints come out when your desires are not met.
And they will spread to those around you
In the form of discontent and grumbling.
For those who practice spiritual training,
Fighting the mind of complaint is also
A difficult virtuous practice.
Why do complaints arise?
The mind of complaint is caused
By the lack of one's own ability.
It is caused by the lack of self-confidence.
Or you may complain when you are tired.
This is natural for human beings.
However,
When you are tired and want to complain,
You should rather remain silent.
When you feel like complaining,
Keep silence and take a deep breath.
Then, work to detach yourself from such thought
As quickly as you can.
Complaint is another poison.
It will harm and pollute your surroundings,

Like scattered trash.
A dump yard will immediately form
Around those who complain.
Who will deal with this dump of complaints?
Who will clean up the trash that was thrown out?
So you must not complain.
If there is no one to clean it up,
You, yourself, who have complained,
Must do something about it.
You must deal with the trash yourself.
If you cannot do so,
You have no choice but to go on living in the dump yard.
This is the terrifying thing about complaining.
When you feel like complaining,
First, encourage your mind.
You must uplift your mind.
You must think, "I am a far greater person."
You must think, "I am created by the Light of Buddha."
You must think,
"I am endowed with the Energy of Buddha."
Encourage yourself
With much more powerful Light.
Then, those feelings of complaint will surely leave you.

Make Efforts in Silence

Another cause that gives rise to complaints
Is concerning unaccomplished desires.
There must be some things you cannot obtain or attain
No matter how hard you are working for them now,
And you may be left with bitter feelings.
However,
What good would come by complaining about it?
Will you make any progress by complaining?
When you row a boat to reach the shore,
Sometimes the water flows back from the shore,
Creating the waves to push your boat further away.
In the same way,
When you have decided to attain something
But failed to do so,
Complaining will only push you further away
From your goal.
It will push your future further away from you.
So instead,
Stop complaining,
And quietly and silently store up power within you.
Look to the future and keep on making efforts

Steadfastly and silently.
No one has ever succeeded without making efforts.
Even if you wish to gain
Easy success without making efforts,
It will by no means benefit your souls.
Such kind of success
Is like building a castle on sand;
It will eventually crumble for sure.
O people, do not spare hard work.
Do not think that you can accomplish things
Without making efforts.
Do not think that you can achieve success
Without making efforts.
If you have achieved success without making efforts,
You should rather be ashamed of that success.
You should rather be ashamed of that honor.
You should rather be ashamed of that fame.
It is not the results
But the process of making efforts itself
That adorns you with the golden glory.
Do not forget this.

I have listed the types of foolish people:
Those who get angry, those who envy,
And those who complain.
This is the Truth in all ages.
Look carefully within your mind,
And always check and see
If you have anger, envy, or complaint.
If you find any of such thoughts,
Remember that you have become one of the fools.
Stop being foolish as quickly as possible,
And become a wise one.
That is the path of those who practice spiritual training.

CHAPTER FOUR

Politics and Economics

All of you, my disciples,
Listen to my words carefully.
In the past,
I told you in many ways
About the mind,
About the teachings of the mind.
And I taught you that
The teachings of the mind always hold true
Beyond time, beyond region, and beyond race.

Within Politics and Economics

However,
All of you, my disciples,
In this age and place where you were born,
There are things you did not learn in the past
Through your spiritual training.
In this current age,
You probably do not know
How to understand politics.
In this current age,
You probably do not know

How to understand economics.
Truly.
In the past,
I did not teach you the way of politics.
In the past,
I did not teach you the way of economics.
In the past,
I taught you to stay away
From politics and economics
And to just seek the peace of mind.
Truly, indeed.
In this age, too,
The highest virtues are, of course,
Peace of mind,
The controlling of the mind,
And the path to enlightenment.
This will never change.

However,
All of you, my disciples,
Living in the framework of
Politics and economics in this age,
How confused and perplexed you must be.

When I see you struggle like this,
I cannot hold back my tears.
My disciples,
Even so, do not be deluded.
Everything that exists in this world
Is the manifestation of the true Will of Buddha
Unfolding in some way or another.
Therefore,
Do not run away from politics in vain.
Do not run away from economics in vain.
Your spiritual training in this lifetime
Should be to show what it means
To live with a pure mind,
A correct mind,
And the peace of mind
And to live in accordance with the Will of Buddha
In the framework of politics and economics.
Yes, the times have changed.
Yet the Eternal Laws will never change.
To spread the Eternal Laws to people,
You must not deny all things of this world.
Strive to discover all the good
That is hidden in this world,

And strive to eliminate all the evil
That arises in this world.
In this effort, you must find the path
Of a true practitioner of spiritual training.

A Spiritual Backbone

All of you, listen carefully.
This nation, Japan,
Where I teach the Laws now,
Has entered an age to lead the world.
However, this country that should lead the world
Does not have a spiritual backbone
On which to base.
This is something to be worried about.
A family will prosper
Only when the head of the household,
Or the master of the home,
Works diligently with a right mind
And unites all the family members.
In the same way,
When a political leader governs a nation

With a pure mind and a right mind,
Staying away from desires and attachments,
Always thinking of the happiness of the people,
And thinking only about making many people happy,
The nation will naturally be governed well
And become peaceful.
However, Japan now has no Laws to devote to.
The nation has no Laws, no teachings to devote to.
This is something deplorable.
I think so.
Do you think that nations are eternal and imperishable?
In fact, they have changed
Depending on the age, the region, and the people.
Even if their names have changed
Or their areas have changed,
Behind them were always
The eternal and imperishable Laws.
There have always been the Eternal Laws.
The Eternal Laws flowed out of Buddha
To faithfully manifest His Will on earth.

The Power to Change the World

All of you, from now on,
You must not just undergo spiritual training.
You must not just live for your spiritual training alone.
Your devotion to spiritual training itself
Must work to awaken the souls of many.
Your spiritual training
And the crowd of you people carrying out
Spiritual training
Must work to change the world.
I believe so.

This society, which is based on desires,
Can only be changed by something
That is not based on desires.
What will change a society disordered by desires
Are the actions of those
Who have freed themselves of attachments.
I believe so.

True attachment is
The aspiration to walk the path to Buddha.

This great, true attachment is recommended
For anyone to have.
On the other hand, false attachment is a mind
That places you only in this earthly world,
Seeks your glories only in this earthly world,
And strives to make your lives easier
Only in this earthly world.
It is important to abandon these false attachments
And have the great attachment, the true attachment,
The attachment to walking toward Buddha.

Perhaps "attachment" is not the right word;
You can replace the word "attachment"
With "affection."
Rather, you could say, strong attraction,
Or the strong power to bond together,
Or the power to improve yourselves
To come infinitely closer to Buddha.

So I tell you,
From now on,
Change the ways of the world,
Change the form of the world,

Change the structure of the world,
By dint of the only power,
By the power to become one with Great Buddha,
And therefore, by the peaceful mind
That is freed from worldly attachments.

To change the world,
Some people may uphold revolution.
Some people may uphold violence.
Some people may uphold blood-shedding.
However, I do not adopt such ideas.
To change the world,
A peaceful mind is essential.
A harmonious mind is essential.
If a nation is overthrown by violence,
The new nation will someday
Be overthrown by violence again.
Revolutions achieved at the cost of blood
Will eventually invite more profuse bleeding.
That is not the way it should be.
In changing the world,
You must definitely value the calm mind.
You must cherish the peaceful mind.

You must change the world by placing value on harmony.
You must change the world
By promoting harmony itself.
You must part from extremes,
Put harmony at the center,
And make it your ideal that everything thrives.

The Truth about Politics

Looking at the politics in Japan today,
I find that the most deplorable point lies here.
Various political parties fight one another,
Each insisting on their own interests.
Some may call this "democracy,"
But I utterly do not think
This way of politics accords with the Will of Buddha.
To truly accord with the Will of Buddha,
All political parties must get together
And seriously think about how they can bring
Light and happiness to the world
And to the minds of people.
They must seriously make proposals to each other.

You must know that democracy based on desires
Is not the true form of politics.
Do not confuse freedom
With arguing over each other's interests
Based on desires.
Freedom should not be the freedom of desires.
Freedom is not about
Letting desires compete with each other.
That must not be taken as true democracy.
There must not be the democracy of desire.
There must not be the democracy of worldly delusions.
You must not choose candidates
For your own political gains,
For your own benefits in life,
Or for your own desires
And let them participate in the politics
Just for these purposes.
Politics must not be that way.
We can say they are doing great in politics
Only when they serve to create a society
That satisfies more and more people—
No, all people.
To achieve this,

It is essential to rid your mind of conflict.
Unless you rid your mind of conflict,
True harmony will not be born.
Many political parties are now fighting with each other.
Do you understand how deplorable this is
From the eyes of Buddha?
Even within the same party,
Different factions dispute with each other
And contend with each other in
Trying to be the party leader.
This may serve the principle of progress in some aspects,
But why does it still make us feel, "Something's wrong"?
This is because people want to avoid leaders
Who favor conflicts and disputes.
From a certain point of view,
The disputes between common people
Could be seen as silly, childish quarrels.
However,
How is it possible for people
To live with a peaceful mind
When they see their leaders
Constantly arguing with each other?
When those who stand above are in conflict,

How can peace be realized below?
How can people harmonize?
How can people be in control of themselves?
This is a sheer contradiction.
It is nothing but a contradiction.
Those who are to stand above others
Must value order and harmony.
Always being exposed to many people's eyes,
They must be virtuous people,
Worthy of many people's respect.
Violent words and actions are unacceptable in the Diet,
Where the nation's politics is debated.
Politicians must restrain themselves
From shameful behaviors as human beings.
Moreover, no matter how much they wish
To win an election,
Or want to expand their power and interests,
They must strictly refrain from words and actions
That try to push others down
Or insult the characters of other people.
You must not call such deeds "freedom of speech."
I believe so.

The poverty of politics is caused
By the poverty of the mind.
Politics is carried out by those
Who are chosen by the people.
If the leaders chosen by the people
Are participating in politics without their hearts,
Then I have to say that
The people who choose them
Are also without their hearts.
That is not the way it should be.
Do politics with a sincere heart.
Choose the leaders
Who will wholeheartedly serve the people.
Choose the leaders who will wholeheartedly act
To make the world a better place.
This is the trend you must create.
Today's politics is to be worried about.
If you do not know whom to choose,
First, choose the ones who are virtuous.
Elect the most virtuous person from among you.
You must not decide by the power of numbers.
You must not decide by the amount of money.
You must not decide by the person's political skills alone.

It is essential to choose the leader
According to how close the person is to Buddha.
In this way,
Never bring factional fighting into politics,
And instead,
Always keep in mind
How to make people wealthier and happier.

The Truth about Economics

In addition,
All of you, my disciples,
You are probably often confused
By today's economic principles.
You probably do not know
How to understand the economic principles themselves.
You probably do not know
How economic principles and Buddha's Truth
Are related to each other.
Many people may be creating suffering
Because of the economy.
Many people may be creating degradation

Because of the economy.

Many people may be creating great attachments

Because of the economy

And may lose their hearts.

However,

If this is the kind of age you live in,

Transcend the economy while living in it.

There should be such a way of living.

No matter how much you refine your minds,

As long as this world is based on

The principles called the "economy,"

You cannot escape them.

If so,

It is essential that you choose the right path

In the frame of these economic principles.

I believe so.

This accords with the right idea

In light of Right Action,

Which I taught in the Eightfold Path.

In the past,

Many of you renounced the world

And lived without ever knowing Right Action.

But now you were born in this age,
And are given the opportunity
To learn what Right Action truly is.
You must thank Buddha for this.
The true Right Action means
Your prospering serves to enrich
The lives of those around you,
And enriching those around you
Serves to enrich the nation as a whole,
Bringing more happiness.
If used correctly,
The principles of the economy will be
The principles to lead many people to happiness.
Indeed, the economy is not just something independent.
The economy must be the driving force
To refine and enrich your minds further.
The economy must serve the mind.
That is how the economy should be.
If your minds start serving the economy,
Or should your minds be enslaved by the economy,
You can no longer say
You are living the life of a human.

All of you,
From now on, beware.
The economy should serve
To make your minds the kings,
And you should not let your minds
Serve the economy.
You must never forget this and only this.
Blessed are those
Who live with a pure mind and prosper.
Those people must use their economic power
As a strength to refine their minds further,
Gain more grounds for training their minds,
And inspire a great number of people.
Those who are financially powerless
Must not greatly suffer from that.
You must not make the economy your suffering.
You must not make it your suffering to be poor.
You must not make it your suffering to fail financially.
Even at such times,
You still have something eternal and imperishable.
You still have the last task
Of refining your eternal and imperishable souls,
Or your minds.

The last task and the first,
And the first task and the last—
That is the task of continuing to refine your minds
No matter what circumstances you are in.
Apply the principles called the "economy"
To the task of continuously refining your minds.
I am sure it is possible
To contribute to the economic principles
While refining your minds and training your souls.
Think about it:
The value measured by money
Should indicate the fact that
If you did work that benefits others,
It will come back to you as your wealth.
This being so,
If you are poor now,
It may be because you did not do
The kind of work that truly enriched other people.
There should also be self-reflection
In terms of economic principles.
Is it possible to remain poor
When you are truly working to benefit others?
If you are truly working to benefit others

But do not become wealthy
And are always in a financial crisis,
It may be because you lack wisdom.
So use your wisdom.
Use your wisdom, and the economy will grow.
Use your wisdom, and the economy will emit light.
Use your wisdom, and you will not fail.
Maybe you are just burning with passion
To achieve your ideals,
Believing that working to truly do good things
Will make you wealthy,
But find yourself in misery
And wonder why it is happening to you.
Most likely,
You are not using your wisdom to the fullest.
What does it mean to use your wisdom?
Using wisdom means to use your time well.
Using wisdom means to use other people well.
Always remember these two points.
Those with wisdom conquer time.
Those with wisdom use their time freely as they like.
They make time their own friend,
And they make time their own weapon.

They make time their own blood,
And they make time their own nutrition.
This is the way of wise people.
There are many examples of people
Who use not only wisdom and time
But also other people to achieve success.
It is important to make the most of other people.
The economy is only possible
When you use people.
The economy is only possible
When you are used by people.
The economy will exert a great power
In studying people,
And it will provide a great ground for the souls.
If you are secluded alone in a temple
And practice Zen meditation all day long,
There is no economic exchange
Or no contact with others there.
But once you go out to the workplace
And do your daily work,
You will be confronted with the question
Of how to make the most of other people
Within the framework of the economic principles.

This will provide you with great lessons.
You must make full use of them.

"It's Enough" Mind

I am sure you have heard of the term,
"The right person in the right place."
It means to place people in a position
That best suits their potentials, talents, and abilities.
The idea of "the right person in the right place"
May be difficult to understand and hard to approve.
The main reason for this is that
People are unable to evaluate themselves correctly
Because they have strong desires.
But you must know the fact that
People feel joy for the first time
When they are being used
In accordance with their potentials.
A saw has a happiness of its own.
A hand plane has a happiness of its own.
A chisel has a happiness of its own.
Do not forget that.

A saw is useful in cutting wood.
Cutting wood well is a joy to a saw.
On the other hand,
Smoothing wood is a joy to a hand plane,
While making grooves in wood is a joy to a chisel.
The saw, hand plane, and chisel are all different
And each is valuable.
Each tool is valuable and indispensable.
However, if people of the world say that
Saws are the best,
All people want to become saws.
If people of the world say that
Hand planes are the best,
Then everyone rushes to become a hand plane.
However, because the world is filled
With many different people
Working in their own positions,
The world becomes better and better.
You may aim to work as a saw
Because it is eye-catching,
But to play the role of a saw,
You need to have strong power.
You need to be bold, decisive, speedy,

And quick to get the job done.
Those with such characteristics
Should take on the role of the saw.
On the other hand, there are others
Who are well-organized,
Love to be of service to others,
And are highly attentive to many people.
These people do not necessarily suit
The role of a saw by their nature.
These people should work
On how to gloss or smooth better as a hand plane.
That is the way to make the most of their true selves.
There are also people
Who dedicate their lives to a specific field.
They may desire to perform
A specific, fine, yet powerful job.
That would be the job of a chisel.
They are useful
In cutting and carving intricate details.
This is what a chisel does.
Some people may scorn such specialized jobs.
Or some of those engaged in such jobs
May have become self-deprecating.

However, such work does exist.
It is difficult to make a tenon using a saw.
It is difficult to make a tenon using a hand plane, too.
You can only do that using a chisel.
So do not forget that
There is a right place for each person.
For this reason,
There are some who become company presidents
And face more difficulties and troubles than others.
It may be a mistake for you to think
That you must deal with them yourself as president
To become happy.
Superiors and subordinates are merely
The hierarchy of this world;
They are not Buddha's true hierarchy.
When every person is placed in the right position,
Everything will get better for the first time.
By no means is fulfilling everyone's desire
A wonderful thing.
If everyone who wanted to be president
Were made as such,
The employees of those companies
Would lose their jobs one after another

And end up facing great suffering.
Know that the person with the potential to be a president
Should be the president.
This being so, never regret the fact that
You are living in accordance with your own capacities.
Of course, those in the position of managing a company
Must be fair in assigning personnel.
And it is right for employees
To desire fair treatment.
However, please remember the analogy I told you
Of the saw, hand plane, and chisel.
Only when these tools are used appropriately,
They become useful and find joy.
They will not find true joy
If used in the wrong place.
Know this well.

To be content is by no means passive.
To be content is to know yourself.
To be content is to know your potential.
To be content is to know your abilities.
To be content is to know your place to live,
To know your path to live,

To find the place to die.
This is the meaning of "It's enough" mind.

Appropriate Progress

Here, I would like to teach you again
The idea of "It's enough" mind.
I feel that this idea is not being applied well enough
Either in the world of politics
Or in the world of economics.
People all seem to be immersed
Only in increasing numbers.
You must know how important this idea is.
It will introduce the principle of harmony
Into the masculine society
In which people are apt to pursue progress only.
By knowing content,
People can be free from extreme ideas.
They can also be free
From the extremes of the top and bottom.
This way of living can be found
In freeing yourself from

The extremes of the left and right,
And the extremes of the top and bottom,
And in the path of entering the Middle Way.
This being so,
This "It's enough" mind must be fully understood
In the world of politics as well.
No matter how much you satisfy your desire for power,
Such a thing serves nothing.
You should understand "It's enough" mind
And think about the way
To make the most of yourself.
The same can be said of the world of economics.
If your company develops,
You may be happy,
But no matter how much it develops,
There is no end.
So the mere expansion of numbers or quantities
Is not necessarily the right thing.
Prosperity and development are righteous
Only when they bring joy to the people
Who belong to them and are living in them.
Never, ever forget that.
"It's enough" mind never means

That you should apply the brakes on progress.
It means that progress must be appropriate.
Unless you consider appropriate progress,
Everything will end in failure.
Even trees should grow appropriately.
Grass and flowers, too, should grow appropriately.
If a sunflower grew to be 30 feet tall,
It would suffer;
How to absorb water from the soil
Would be its pressing need, anxiety, and suffering.
So for sunflowers,
Six feet would be the appropriate height.
Some people may think differently.
They would be happy if a persimmon tree, for example,
Bears much fruit.
However, think about what would happen
If the tree bears too much fruit.
The branches of the tree would bend
By the weight of the fruit,
Deteriorating the taste of the fruit.
Deteriorating the taste means
The tree has worked in vain.
Bearing much fruit

Will not necessarily bring joy to people.
If the fruit loses its taste,
People will no longer be happy about it.
So it is best that a tree bears delicious fruit
In an appropriate amount.
It is not right that the harvest be bountiful at times
And poor at other times,
Fluctuating right and left, or up and down.
Always bearing the right amount of persimmons
With the right taste,
While never failing to meet the expectations of people,
Is the right thing.
Do not forget this idea.
The right amount is essential for any success.
In all things,
You must neither overdo
Nor underdo.
The Middle Way is, by no means,
A way to temporary success;
It is the way to achieve boundless success.
Now, think back on your work;
Always check and see
If there is anything that is not in the right amount.

Examining anything that is not in the right amount
Is equal to entering the Middle Way.
One of the ways to enter this Middle Way
Is the perspective of "It's enough" mind.
Do not forget this.
People are apt to put on a good face
And try to appear good.
They seek superficial success
And go after easy money.
But frivolous profit, frivolous glory, frivolous vanity—
These things will never truly enrich your souls.
Do not forget that.

Progress from the Middle Way

In times of success,
Think about things modestly.
In times of failure,
Live as you encourage your minds.
Both are ways to enter the Middle Way
Without going into the extremes.
In times of success,

Foolish people will expand their ego,
Become haughty and arrogant,
And repeat words without any respect for others.
Then, eventually,
When their environment gets worse,
They sink into the depths of failure all too easily,
And there is no one left to help them.
But in the depths of despair,
If you become self-deprecating
And keep on complaining,
No one would want to accompany you, either.
If we accompany those who keep on complaining,
Our minds will be darkened as well.
So it is also a wise road
To avoid socializing with people who darken our minds.
Those who choose such a wise road will not associate
With people who grumble and complain
In the depths of despair.
Therefore, even if you are in the depths of despair,
Encourage your minds
And try to live with strength
In search of the light of hope.
As you take the powerful first step,

Then the next step,
And are about to take the third step,
You will gradually gain the recognition
Of those around you,
Enabling you to return to the Golden Road
Of the wonderful Middle Way.
This is how success is.
O people,
Always keep the Middle Way.
Keep the Middle Way,
And keep in mind the progress from the Middle Way.
In politics and in economics,
Keep the Middle Way,
And keep in mind the progress from the Middle Way.
This is the way for you
To harm no people,
Love all people,
And bring happiness to all people.

The Middle Way for a Nation

Until now,
You may have thought that
The principle of the Middle Way
Is the principle of the mind
For you and for each individual.
You may have taken the principle of the Middle Way
As the principle of the mind only
And understood the principle of the Middle Way
As the Hinayana principle only.
However, the principle of the Middle Way
Goes beyond the level of Hinayana
And applies to the level of Mahayana as well.
Just as the Middle Way of living is important
For each and every person's life,
The Middle Way is and will be
Just as important on a large scale,
Such as for societies and nations.
In international relations, too,
Conflicts between nations suddenly have surfaced now,
Creating serious problems.
At times like this,

You must have a standard for your ways of thinking.
The standard for your ways of thinking
Must be the Middle Way.
The biggest key to coordinating the interests
Between Japan and the U.S.,
Or Japan and any other nation,
Is to be found in the Middle Way.
You are apt to think that
Just pushing for ways to seek
The interests of your own nation
And to reject the interests of other nations
Will lead to the prosperity of your own nation only,
But that won't be the result.
If your nation is the only one to prosper,
With other nations declining more and more,
Then international trade will become impossible.
Only when
Both your nation and other nations prosper
Will the world become a wonderful place
For the first time
And will the wonderful international economy
Emerge for the first time.
You must not mistake this point.

Do not seek the interests of your country,
Of your own nation only.
Japan has now become narrow-minded.
Being narrow-minded,
It has been showing a tendency to seek its interests only.
It should not be that way.
Japan must have a heart of great love.
It must pay more respect
To those who were ahead of us
And trained and guided our country in the past.
It must also give a lot more love as a teacher
To the countries that follow behind,
With Japan as their aim, their ideal.
It must devote itself to educating others as a teacher.
It must devote itself to guiding others as a teacher.
That is what Japan should naturally do.
Do not forget the favors
That the developed nations did to Japan in the past.
Because the countries called developed nations
Taught Japan their philosophy, culture,
And economic principles
Was Japan able to develop until today.
This being so,

Japan must think about how to return the favors
When it stands in the position to guide others.
If Japan has surpassed those who were once ahead of it,
It must not forget to remain respectful of them.
It must do what it can for them.
It must not feel too proud
For having surpassed their powers.
It must not become arrogant.
What is more,
Can Japan bring many benefits
To the countries that strive to catch up to it,
Just as the developed nations did for Japan?
Having surpassed the rival developed nations,
If Japan, in turn, becomes fearful
And hesitates to provide help, support,
And education to developing nations,
Then that is self-preservation as a nation.
All the principles of prosperity and development
Are to be found in the Middle Way
And in the progress from the Middle Way.
Do not forget these things.
You must take a big, global view
And think about politics and economics

From the perspective of the theory of the Middle Way.
Never, ever be overly concerned
About the interests of your country alone,
The benefits of your country alone.
Do not forget that
Only when you help others prosper
Will you prosper as well.
Strongly, strongly
I want to tell you this.

CHAPTER FIVE

Patience and Success

All of you, my disciples,
Today I am going to tell you about
The topic of patience and success.
This is a very important topic.

Walk Silently

I have always taught you
To abandon your attachments.
The biggest attachment of all
That keeps you away from success
Is your attachment to time.
Your attachment to time means impatience.
You are always suffering
From the attachment called "impatience."
You are always deluded
By the attachment called "impatience."
You are always enslaved
By the attachment called "impatience."

O people,
Impatience, indeed, is an enemy of life.

Those who go silently will travel far.
Those who go with less noise
Will run a thousand miles.
If you walk loudly
With the sounds of gongs and drums,
You cannot travel very far
Because crowds of people will flock around you
Upon hearing the banging and beating
Of the gongs and drums,
And as you get deep into conversation with them,
You will eventually forget
The original purpose of your journey.

Therefore, all of you,
If you are to hurry on your journey,
Go silently.
If your destination lies far ahead,
Go right away.
You should go profoundly and silently.
At that time,
You must never be impatient.
You must never be hasty.
Have you ever thought about what impatience is?

Impatience means the desire to get results
As quickly as possible.
It is the desire to get the fruit of your effort
Earlier than others
While sparing your own effort.

Therefore, all of you,
Strongly keep this in mind:
When your minds waver in life,
Ask yourselves
If it is actually nothing but impatience,
If impatience has given rise to your doubt,
Or if impatience is the root cause of your doubt.
At that time,
Breathe deeply and ask yourselves
Why you are so impatient.
Why are you impatient?
Why are you in a rush?
Why are you in a fluster?
Think about it,
And you will realize there is no real reason.
There is no real reason, indeed.
The root cause of impatience is always the same;

You are impatient for no real reason.
It means you have a vague feeling
That something terrible might happen to you in time.
You are anxious that something terrible might occur
To harm you in the future.
In most cases,
Impatience arises because you are overwhelmed
By the shadows of anxiety.
The root cause of impatience is to be found in the anxiety
That something that harms you or hurts you
Will confront you.

All of you, think hard
About where lies your life's mission
And where lies your life's purpose.
Then, I am sure you will hit upon a fact:
By no means
Are we aiming to live through life on earth
As quickly as possible.
Even if you manage to run through your life in a rush,
Such a life has no flavor to it.
Even if you manage to attain the peak of your growth,
Such a thing is nothing special.

Do not fear that your life is uneventful.
Do not fear that your life is ordinary.
Do not let your mind waver by temporary trends.
Do not give in to the common sense of the world.
Do not be deluded by the opinions of the public.
Also,
Do not be deluded by the feelings
Of even those who say they love you deeply.

Those who go on the Path must go silently.
Those who walk the Path must go silently.
Do not let others notice your footsteps.
You do not need to tell others
That you are going on a long journey.
No, you must not tell others.
If you tell others
That you are going on a long journey,
Some may try to stop you.
They do not necessarily do so out of an ill will.
Some may do so out of goodwill.
There will be no end to the people
Who advise you not to go on a long journey,
Saying it is quite dangerous.

A Time of Loneliness

However, all of you, my disciples,
You are already walking the path of spiritual training.
If you are already walking the path of spiritual training,
Be strong in your mind.
Be prepared to endure this long journey alone.
Build up the strength to endure loneliness.
The key to the victory in life
Indeed lies here, in enduring loneliness.
Those who fail in enduring loneliness
Have never experienced true success.
That is because everyone will experience
A moment of loneliness
Before achieving true success.
A cheerful time may come
After this time of loneliness.
But the truth is always one:
A time of loneliness always precedes success.
The question is
How you have lived through this time of loneliness.

At times, this loneliness before success
Ends after a short period of time,
But at other times, it lasts for long.
Some may live in loneliness
For 10 years or even 20 years.
However, do not be afraid;
Do not fear loneliness.
Do not forget that
Buddha stands by you
When you are lonely.
Do not forget that
The Great One has also come down
And is sitting close to you
When you are sitting alone.

You are not alone.
You are not just being alone.
You are now forging your souls in the real sense.
Light is about to shine from your souls now.
Your souls are about to shed inner light.
O young ones,
Do not fear loneliness.
It is exactly in loneliness

That a chance is found for your souls to grow.
How you endure this time of real loneliness
Is a chance to test your true potential.
O young ones,
Do not only seek cheerful times.
Do not only seek to live in bustle among others.
Do not only hope to draw the attention of others
Or gain admiration from others.
In times of loneliness,
There is something that will nurture you eternally.
Grasp this "something"
That will nurture you eternally.
When you grasp this "something eternal,"
You will change.
No, you cannot help but change.
You will experience a 180-degree turnabout.
And you shall meet the great time,
Great moment, and great life.
Only when this loneliness is overcome
Will a truly brave one be born.

The Road to Success

Now, I will tell you yet another thing.
I am sure you are fascinated by success.
I am sure that every day
You are enamored with success.
I am sure that every day
You think about what success is.
However, success is perhaps far different
From what you think it is.
Or success may actually lie very close to you.
There is no clear definition for success.
However, I tell you:
There are elements that can never be neglected
For you to say you have become truly successful.

1) Always Have a Peaceful Mind

As a condition of success,
If your mind is disturbed by your success,
You cannot call it a success.
Your mind must always be peaceful and poised.

Your mind must always be calm
And free of attachments.
If, by achieving success,
You end up having more and more attachments,
Then it is not true success.
I think so.
If, by achieving success,
Your mind becomes more and more peaceful
And calmer and calmer,
Always carrying wealth
To the point where you can think about many people,
Success becomes real.
I believe so.

2) Do Not Invite Envy

In the process of achieving success,
If you create various emotional conflicts,
Create attachments,
Or invite grudge and envy,
Then that is not true success.
That is why,

As the second condition of success,
I tell you:
Do not invite the envy of others.
Not a single person has achieved great success
By inviting other people's envy.
Some people may appear to have achieved success
At a glance,
But many of those who invited other people's envy
Eventually sank into the depths of their downfall.
Truly.
The fact that you have invited the envy of others
Means that your success was actually achieved
By pushing down on other people's heads.
Your success was built on other people's shoulders.
You forced others to carry heavy burdens
For you to achieve your own success.
If your success serves
To carry the burden of other people,
Make other people's lives easier,
And make other people happier,
Then your success will never invite the envy of others.
It will never invite the grudge of others.
However, if there is even one person

Who envies your success,
Then you must think that
You are still lacking in virtue.
You are still far from being virtuous.
What does it mean to lack in virtue?
It means
There are people who feel they suffered a loss
Because of your success.
There are people
Who feel your success is unfair.
There are people
Who feel they can hardly approve of your success.
This is not the kind of success you should aim for.
True success must be something
That is naturally supported and propelled
By the people around you.
True success should be a natural result
Rather than an intended one.
True success must be truly appreciated
By many people.
There is no such thing as true success
That is not appreciated by many.
I believe so.

3) Give Off the Fragrance of Enlightenment

I will tell you the third condition of success as well.
So far, I have told you that
It is essential to have a peaceful mind
And the attitude of not inviting others' envy.
In addition to these,
There is another important attitude for success.
What can it be?
It is that your souls must shine more brightly.
Do you understand what it means
For your souls to shine more brightly?
It means that you must give off
The fragrance of enlightenment around you.
You must give off
A scent of enlightenment around you.
What is the fragrance of enlightenment
Or the light of the soul?
Do you understand what it is?
I tell you:
The fragrance of enlightenment
Is not something you can gain by pursuing it.

It is not something you can obtain by taking it.
By no means is it such things.
The fragrance of enlightenment
Is gained without taking
And is gained without desiring to have it.
It is just like a butterfly
That flies high up into the sky
To escape your net
When you chase to catch it
But naturally comes down
To sit and rest on your shoulder
When you stand still.
In the same way,
Enlightenment comes quite naturally,
Contrary to your will.
And it will enrich you and the people around you
With its mellow fragrance.

Let me tell you the meaning of this teaching
From a different viewpoint.

The Melody of a Leaf Flute

Once upon a time, there was a giant.

The giant was about eight feet tall. When he would walk around the village, everyone trembled in fear upon seeing his face; they would run into their houses, bolt their doors, and peek out from the window gaps to see him walk away. The giant always wrapped a turban around his head and wore a gold band on his arm. His skin was the color of fiery bronze, and he wore filthy gray trousers. The iron shackle around his ankle suggested he had escaped from somewhere.

The giant was very strong; dragging a horse or two was a piece of cake. With his tremendous power, he could crush a small wooden house all too easily. When the giant passed by, even animals ran about screaming in fear of being strangled by him.

So the elders of the village got together and held a discussion.

"What to do with that giant? We must somehow stop his brutal acts. Is there any way?"

The elders of the village discussed for three days and three nights but came up with no answer.

"We can't come up with an answer, but if we succeed in capturing that giant and forcing him out of the village, things may work out for now."

One of the elders suggested this, to which others responded, "Yes, if we can capture that giant and force him out of the village, then surely we will be safe. But what if he comes back?"

"That's right. We wouldn't know when he would come back, and that would worry us even more."

"But how do we capture this giant alive in the first place? Is there anyone who has the courage to do so?" asked another.

"Well, maybe it's better we dare to kill the giant if we don't want him to come back, even if it would mean for us to commit the sin of killing."

The discussion continued like this for a while: How can we kill the giant? He would go on a rampage and might kill dozens of villagers if we failed to kill him. Even if we shoot an arrow, we never know if it would truly pierce that robust body; even if it did, it might just be a scratch to that giant. Setting a trap to capture him is one option, but if he finds out, it would cause us another big trouble.

The elders discussed hundreds of plans, but not a single good idea came to them.

"What to do?" "What should we do?"

Just then, a young woman, who was listening to the elders, spoke up.

"I'm not sure if you'd listen, but I have a good idea. Please consider trying my idea."

The elders were taken by surprise. How could such a young woman get rid of that giant? They had no idea.

But the woman insisted, "Please count on me. I will definitely put an end to the giant's brutal acts tomorrow, and we will no longer have trouble after that."

"Well, if you can do such a thing, then that would be great. What do you think, fellows?"

The elders discussed it with each other but because they had no better ideas, they finally decided to take up her plan and entrust her with the problem.

This young woman had a young son. He was as young as about five years. He was not particularly special in any way, but there was one thing he was good at—the art of blowing a leaf flute. This wise, young mother was convinced that the giant would surely become calm by listening to her son's leaf flute.

The next day, from the outskirts of the village, the giant came tramping again toward the central area, kicking up a lot of sand. The villagers closed their storm shutters again and were hiding in their houses, frightened. Which place will suffer damage today? Who will be hurt? Thinking like this, they were all trembling in fear. There stood just the mother and her son at the center of the village. Seeing them in the open space, people worried and whispered to each other. "Are they okay? That's only a young woman and a child. They wouldn't last a second. Maybe they would be eaten up."

Then, the ogre-looking giant arrived. As everyone worried, he almost grabbed the mother and the child. Everyone gulped in fear.

"Oh, this is going to be terrible!"

But then the mother gently nodded to her child, standing to her right with a calm look on her face. The child then took a blade of grass from his pocket and started to play it.

Peep tu-re-lu-re-lu. Peep tu-re-lu-re-lu.

The melody of the leaf flute reminded the giant of some indescribable feeling.

"Wow, this sound! What is this sound? Oh, I know this sound. I'm sure I've heard it somewhere. Where did I hear it?"

The mother saw through him. The giant must have come from somewhere around India. He must have been a servant of a nobleman. The nobleman most probably used music to calm the brutal character of this man. She perceived so.

Indeed, the giant had been serving a young lord in the past before he escaped. His young lord was not so big, but he would play the flute beautifully to tame the giant. That is why, upon hearing the leaf flute played by the young boy, the giant remembered the melody he had missed for a long time.

And this prompted the giant to reflect on all he had done to this day. Then, large teardrops began trickling down his face, one after another.

The villagers were amazed. "Look, the giant shed tears at the melody of the five-year-old boy's leaf flute!"

"Oh well, the giant wasn't such a bad man after all. Look at him crying at the melody of a child's leaf flute. He wasn't such a bad man."

Cautiously, they began to open their shutters, and out came one villager, then two, eventually filling the open space with a lot of people.

"Oh, I see, we thought that there was nothing good about this giant, but he has a sense for music. Why not play the flutes together, then?"

The villagers each brought a flute, and they all played it. The giant, who was at first shedding tears, gradually became joyful and started to dance with the villagers. Thus, through the melody of the flutes, the kind heart of the giant was recognized, the people around him felt relieved, and they learned to live together in peace.

The giant protected the village from foreign enemies, and the villagers soothed his mind by playing their flutes.

As such, they both lived peacefully ever after.

Enlightenment within the Ordinary

Now, do you understand what I wanted to tell you
Using this allegory?
The giant and the villagers
Are not separate individuals.
They are actually both inhabitants of your own mind.

In fact, in your mind reside
An uncontrollable, brutal giant
And a cowardly self
That trembles in fear of the giant.
Everyone has both in their mind.
I am sure you have a mind
That is inevitably drawn by desires
No matter how hard you may try to control it.
The mind that is drawn by desires is, for example,
A mind that goes crazy
Upon seeing someone of the opposite sex,
A mind that goes crazy
Upon seeing money,
A mind that goes crazy
Upon seeing other people's possessions,

Or a mind that is disturbed
Upon hearing of someone becoming happy.
I am sure there is such an uncontrollable "something,"
Like a raging storm,
Lying within you.
This uncontrollable "something" is, in fact,
The giant in the story.
However, even this uncontrollable giant
Still has fond memories of being controlled,
Governed, and tamed by someone, somewhere,
When he was once chained.
If you make him recall these fond feelings,
That is to say,
If you let him hear the nostalgic melody of the flute,
You can tame the giant.
Controlling the giant is something that can be done
By even a small villager,
Who is regarded as a much weaker person.

Truly—
First, you must rid yourself of fear.
Do not think that
Your mind is beyond your control.

Do not think that
You are someone who can be manipulated
Or controlled by evil,
As if you are not yourself.
You must think that
You can definitely control your own mind.
And the way to control your mind
Is by no means through physical strength.
It is not by threatening or hurting your mind.

Do you understand what I mean by this?
I am telling you that
You cannot control your mind
By undergoing difficult and ascetic training.
There are different types of difficult and ascetic training,
Such as meditating under a waterfall or fasting.
But attempting to tame and control your mind
Through difficult or ascetic training
Is like trying to capture the giant
By shooting arrows or setting traps;
It will only drive the giant to act more brutal.
The mind will become even more out of control.

It shouldn't be that way.
The mind can be governed
In a more peaceful way,
Using a much smaller discovery,
In a more enjoyable manner.
What I want to say is this:
By no means
Is enlightenment found in the extraordinary world.
By no means
Is enlightenment found in extraordinary experiences.
In fact, the moment for enlightenment
Is found within your ordinary, everyday lives.
In fact, that is where the path to enlightenment is.
And the enlightenment that you find
In your ordinary days, in each of your ordinary days,
Actually lies in a very small discovery.
This is what I want to say.

What is this "very small discovery"?
It is the melody we knew
When we were in the Real World
Or the heavenly world.
It is to recall that melody.

In order for us to attain enlightenment,
We need to recall the melody we enjoyed
In the Real World.
This is important.
What is this melody we enjoyed in the Real World?
It is a kind feeling toward others;
It is the heart of congratulating others;
It is a mind that restrains desires from growing
Or an "It's enough" mind.
Or it is the attitude of harmonizing with each other,
Helping each other,
And bringing up each other.
It is by no means
The mind that seeks the happiness of yourself only
Or the attitude of insisting on your selfish desires.
We must have had such an attitude.
We must have had such a feeling
That was crystal clear, boundlessly kind,
And infinitely warm.

Indeed, such a world is heaven.
Even when you come down and live on earth
As you do now,

Live each day remembering this heaven.
Live every day
While visualizing the life in heaven.
Then, it is the same
As blowing a very small leaf flute.
Always imagine the peaceful world as you live.
At that time, the giant will calm down
And will no longer be your enemy.
He will become a very precious power
That stands on your side
And acts at your will.

Patience and Virtue

Just now, I told you something very ordinary.
I told you that the fragrance of enlightenment
Lies in the ordinary.
Now, do you understand the relationship between
This fragrance of enlightenment
Or this sensation of your souls emitting light,
Which is the condition of success,
And patience?

In fact, patience and success are bridged
By the word "ordinary."
Patience may not play so big of a role
In the extraordinary days of an extraordinary life.
However, it takes infinite patience
To keep on living an ordinary life day after day.
Leading an ordinary life every day
Requires infinite patience.
In every age, it is difficult and challenging
To imagine the nostalgic scenes of heaven
From time to time
And live with them as your ideals
While leading an ordinary life every day.

However, these untiring efforts
Will allow people to keep making progress forever.
It is difficult to attain sudden enlightenment
In the process of spiritual training.
It is difficult to make great progress all of a sudden.
Even if you cannot read an entire book,
Read at least a single line
So that you can feel you have taken a step forward today.
Accumulating such a day each day

Is actually the key to opening the way to a great future.
Patience is necessary for success.
And success achieved with patience
Will never invite the envy of others.
That is because
The amount of effort spent to achieve success
Earns the respect of other people.
In this way,
Success achieved through patience
Will always shine with virtue.
This virtue has an antidote
That can completely clear away
Other people's jealousy and bitterness.
All successful people
Must acquire virtue through patience.
That is important.
Then, your efforts will definitely be rewarded
With further blessings.
I am sure great influence will be born from your virtue.
I believe so.

CHAPTER SIX

What Is Reincarnation?

All of you, my disciples,
Today I will tell you about
Something you have long forgotten.

The Philosophy of Reincarnation

You must have learned about reincarnation
On many occasions in the past.
However, it has been long
Since the philosophy of reincarnation
Became ancient on earth.
No, rather than ancient,
It is more accurate to say that
It is taken as a mere allegory of the past
Or as a funny story.
And sadly,
Even Buddhist monks and nuns,
Who are the inheritors of my teachings,
May not take reincarnation as truth.
No, I am rather concerned that
The majority of them do not believe in it now.

All of you, my disciples,
You must be serious in studying the Truth.
Having been born in this lifetime,
Each of you has different ways of thinking.
Your ways of thinking have been formed
Based on the education you have received
And the various experiences you have had.

However, I say to you:
This world is an extremely severe training ground
For your enlightenment.
You, who have always descended with me onto earth,
Have always chosen to be born
Into difficult environments.
However,
The land of Japan in my current lifetime
Seems to be under much severer conditions
Than the land of India in my previous lifetime.
In the land of India,
There was a tradition of revering Buddha and God.
There was also a tradition
Of believing in the world after death.
In the land of Japan today,

Although the same traditions still remain,
They have no substance.
Many of those who mock the world after death
And the reincarnation of human beings
Do not have the will to learn the Truth for themselves
But try to judge things
Based solely on the knowledge and experiences
They have acquired after birth.
However, just how much Truth can be found
In that knowledge and those experiences?

All of you, my disciples,
Listen to my words carefully.
You must not be afraid in this lifetime.
You must not be daunted.
You must not be overwhelmed.
Do not think about how to make your lives easier.
Do not think too much about it.

All of you, my disciples,
Are you proud to be Buddha's disciples?
Are you proud to live for the Truth?
Are you proud to live for Buddha's Truth?

If you still have not lost the pride
Of living for the Truth,
Then listen to me carefully.

People on earth mock the world after death.
And they want to ignore it.
If they see someone speaking of the afterworld,
They call that person crazy.
Or they call that person weird.
This makes life on earth very difficult
For people who have a right mind, a pure mind,
And good knowledge of the true world.
At times, these people are ridiculed, slandered,
Denounced, or reviled.

Some will experience such hardships
For believing my words.
However, I say to you:
Even if you are hurt for my sake,
Those wounds shall someday bring you great glory.
Even if you are humiliated for my sake,
Those feelings of shame shall someday bring you
Great rewards in heaven.

Even if you should die for my sake,
Your great thoughts shall move various deities of heaven
To tears of great joy.

All of you, my disciples,
You must not think too much about your reputation.
You must not be too self-conscious.
You must not think too much
About gaining people's respect on earth.
You must happily put yourself
In a position others do not respect.
You must happily put yourself
In a position others disdain—
For the only Buddha's Truth,
For the only teachings of Buddha.
You have always learned my teachings
In the process of tens, hundreds,
Or thousands of incarnations.
And every time you received my teachings,
You have gone through
An infinite number of hardships and difficulties.
You are such strong people,
So why should you hesitate now?

Why should you fear now?
Why should you now—
Why should you now?

All of you, my disciples,
You are so dear to me.
You are infinitely darling to me.
I cannot stand to see you suffer.
I cannot stand to silently see you weep.
If you are hurt, in worry, and suffering
For abiding by my teachings,
Know that I, too, am worrying and suffering
Together with you.
I shall not fail to find your tears.
I will surely be suffering with you.
I will surely be worrying with you.
I will surely be carrying huge suffering
Upon my shoulders with you.

Knowing Preciousness

All of you, my disciples,
Indeed, there is no mistake in my teachings of the Truth,
No matter how great a power on earth may deny them,
Even if someone of the highest social status on earth
May deny them,
Even if the wisest person on earth may deny them.
Human beings have eternal souls
And are going through cycles of reincarnation.
Not a single person can deny this Truth.
Denying this Truth is equal
To denying the Will of Buddha
And denying the existence of Buddha.
Denying the existence of Buddha is equal
To denying the world Buddha created
And denying the human beings Buddha created.
It means that
Human beings deny human beings themselves.

However, think about it:
It is something to be ashamed of.
Why do you fear to believe that

Human beings are created by Buddha
And are endowed with eternal souls?
Why does it sound strange to you?
Why does it sound absurd to you?
What is so precious in believing
Human beings have evolved from amoebas?
What is so precious in believing
Human beings are made up of lumps of matter?
Do not say such foolish things.
If these were true,
How can we say human beings are precious?
Humans are precious
Because of the entity that dwells inside of them.
The entity that dwells in human beings indicates that
All beings are energies separated from Buddha;
They are lives created by Buddha.
This is what makes human beings precious.
Those who cannot understand this preciousness
Can never understand any good;
They can never understand any beauty;
They can never understand any truth.
Humans who never understand any good, any beauty,
And any truth

Are no longer human beings despite being humans.
They just retain human shape.
The most important thing
As you are born on earth and living as a human
Is to know what is precious.
It is to perceive something precious
Out of various experiences on earth.
It is to strongly, strongly feel
How precious it is for you to be allowed to live,
How precious it is for other life forms
To be allowed to live,
And how precious the world of Buddha's creation is.

The Greatest Truth

All of you, my disciples,
I am very sad.
You seem to fear greatly to be called a religion.
You seem to fear greatly that
People might call you blind believers or fanatic believers.
However, I say to you:
Fact is fact; truth is truth.

Not a single person can distort this.
Even if someone may ridicule, deny,
Criticize, or slander you,
Know that they do not know anything.
Those who do not know anything
Cannot criticize you, who know the Truth.
People cannot say
More than what they know.
Their understanding of things
Is their limit to how much they can express.

Even if people are born
Into the same age, in the same region,
And in a similar position,
Their souls are at different levels.
That is because through the process of eternal evolution,
Some have advanced more quickly
While others have walked behind slowly.
This fact is hardly perceived while being on earth.
No, in fact,
The truth is often perceived as the opposite.
People who find it easy to live earthly lives,
People who wish to make earthly lives easier,

And people who wish to live better earthly lives
Are apt to be given important positions.
For this reason,
People who believe in another world
And who wish for the happiness of another world
May find it difficult to live in this world.

However, summon your courage.
Those who know the Truth must be strong.
Those who know the Truth
Must not be weak in their minds.
Do not succumb to the irresponsible criticism
Of other people.
Do not succumb to the criticism
Of those who can only understand things
In a superficial way.
Truth is truth; fact is fact.
Do not let the common sense of the world serve forever
As common sense.

All of you, my disciples,
There is at least one thing I must tell you.
As your bare minimum work,

You need to teach people
That human beings have eternal lives
And that they reincarnate between this world
And another world.
This philosophy is, in fact,
The greatest Truth people can discover
In the process of being born, living,
And growing as human beings.
No matter how many earthly truths you may learn,
Nothing is more valuable than this Truth.
They are nothing but mere childish tricks
From the perspective of this Truth.
The fact that human beings live an eternal life
And repeatedly reincarnate—
When people come to know this fact,
Their sense of values must definitely change.
They will see their sense of values
Make a 180-degree turn.
In other words,
After knowing that fact,
People can think about their lives
Within the span of a much longer time.

The Blessed

Blessed are those
Who can believe in another world
And believe in reincarnation
Without ever being compelled by others,
Without ever being forced,
Or without ever being really taught.
These people retain in their souls
The memories of how they had lived in their past lives.
They have memories of Buddha's Truth
In the relatively shallow part of their souls.
These people are blessed.
They must have had many opportunities
To learn and assimilate Buddha's Laws
In their past incarnations as well.
These people have learned Buddha's Truth
In their past incarnations,
And precisely because of that,
They must have come to understand the Truth
At a relatively early stage
In this lifetime as well.

All of you, my disciples,
I believe it has not been long
Since you entered the path of spiritual training.
Even so,
You have arrived at Buddha's Truth
At such an early stage,
Gained the connection to Buddha's Truth,
And become able to walk the path to enlightenment.
So be grateful for that.
It is the greatest happiness of being born as humans
To arrive at Buddha's Truth,
To gain the connection to Buddha's Truth,
And to have started to walk the path
Leading to enlightenment.
You must tell yourselves again and again
That you are blessed people.

No matter how much earthly wealth is piled before you,
No matter how much earthly fame is piled before you,
No matter how many earthly positions, titles,
Or powers—
All of such things are piled before you,
They can never match this happiness.

You must not hand over this happiness
Even in exchange for all earthly happiness
Or for gold, silver, and jewels.
The happiness of those
Who have gained the connection to Buddha's Truth
And are walking the path of enlightenment
Cannot be replaced by anything.
Having entered the path of Buddha's Truth
And entered the path to attain enlightenment,
If you want to keep your happiness to the end,
You must be free from all fear.

You must abandon financial fears.
You must abandon fears of not being loved by others.
You must abandon fears of not being respected by others.
You must not fear
That you will no longer be called great people.
That is not how you should be.
As you walk this path to enlightenment,
If you have realized how precious this happiness is,
Nothing in this world will matter to you anymore.
You must know this.
Those things will eventually pass;
They will eventually fade away and disappear.

The Road to Happiness

Therefore,
All of you, my disciples,
As you live on earth,
If your minds waver in various ways,
Or if you struggle to make a decision on various occasions,
First choose the way
That allows you to further pursue
The path of enlightenment.
Choose to walk in that direction.
Do not think too much about other things.
Do not think too much
About your livelihood, positions, or fame.
Even if you let go of these things,
They will come back to you again someday.
However,
Should you abandon the path of enlightenment,
It is extremely difficult to return to that path.

All of you, my disciples,
I tell you again and again.
Remember these words of mine.
Do you know how difficult it is

To be born in the same age as Buddha?
Being born in the same age as
When Buddha descended on earth
Is the greatest happiness beyond description.
Blessed are those who were able to be born
In such an age,
In such a region,
And in the same generation as Buddha.
And blessed are those
Who could encounter Buddha while alive.
Blessed are those who could encounter Buddha,
Hear Buddha's voice,
And witness Buddha while alive.
This happiness is probably worth the happiness
Of tens of millions or hundreds of millions of years.

It is also difficult to be born
In the age of Buddha's descent,
To encounter Buddha in the age of Buddha's descent,
To hear Buddha's teachings,
And to attain enlightenment
Based on Buddha's teachings
Or through having such a connection.

You must know that
Being able to do so is rare happiness.
Even simply being born in the same age as Buddha
Is a rare chance.
Being able to encounter Buddha while alive, also,
Is a rare chance,
Let alone
Being able to encounter Buddha
And being granted enlightenment—
It is a chance that hardly ever occurs.
To attain this great happiness,
You must be ready to give up all things.
You must enter that path
Even if it costs you to abandon all other things.
This is something you must never forget.
Various attachments that you cling onto in this world
Will become completely meaningless
When you leave this world.
You cannot take those things with you
To another world.
No matter who you are,
It is difficult to live longer than 100 years.
What can you take with you

When you leave this world?
Know that your mind is the only thing
You can take with you.
If your mind is the only thing you can take with you,
Then there is nothing else you should do
But fill your mind with happiness.
The best way to fill your mind with happiness
Is to taste the joy of enlightenment.
If you have tasted the joy of enlightenment
And filled your mind with happiness,
Then you can say that
Your life this time was a success.
To attain this happiness,
Stake everything.

Everyday Discoveries, Everyday Excitement

However, I tell you:
There are many people
Who are determined to live like that for a while.

It is not so difficult to have determination for a while
To devote one's life to Buddha, to Buddha's teachings,
And to attaining enlightenment.
However, most probably,
Eight or nine people out of ten
Will eventually forget that passion
And sink into their ordinary lives.
Remember that
When you have forgotten that passion
And how precious such a life is,
You have already fallen
And are just counting stones
At the riverbank named ordinary.
Listen,
The path of spiritual training
Is the path of everyday discoveries
And everyday excitement.
If you can no longer feel these things,
Then I have to say you have already become conceited.
The conceited cannot pass through
The entrance gate to enlightenment.
The conceited will be expelled from that gate.

They will stumble out of the gate
And eventually will have no choice
But to return the way they came.

All of you, my disciples,
All life's victories are determined like that.
Everyone can have a resolution for a while.
However,
It is difficult to stick to it.
Those who have succeeded in sticking to their resolve
Shall reach yet a greater state of mind.
When you have reached this state of indomitable resolve,
Both Heaven and Earth will celebrate it.

This Life and the Afterlife

All of you, my disciples,
Keep on listening to my words.
Your happiness is not limited to this lifetime alone.
The happiness you enjoyed in this world in this lifetime
Clearly shows the kind of place that awaits you
In another world

When you leave this world.
The state of mind you have attained in this lifetime
Will determine the realms of the world
You will inhabit in the afterlife.
You may have already studied that
Different realms exist in the world called heaven.
At the bottom there is, of course, the world called hell.
Above hell is another world of delusion,
Inhabited by those who are still lost.
Above that is the world of good people,
And yet above that is the world of great high spirits.
The world is divided into different layers,
Or dozens of layers,
And even the inhabitants of the other world
Do not know all those detailed segmentations.
However, this is the truth.
The world you call the heavenly world
Is made up of many layers,
Clearly classifying the state of the human mind.

While you were living on earth,
Various outcomes were produced
By the quality of your physical bodies

Or by the self-realization achieved
Using your physical bodies.
But what awaits you in the afterlife
Is simply the manifestation
Of the level of your mind.
If you have a higher state of mind,
You will go to a higher world,
And if you have a lower state of mind,
You will go to a lower world.
Know that there are no other criteria.
But one thing you must be wary of is
That those who go to hell are not just those
Who were unsuccessful in this world.
There are many people who have gone to hell
Despite being successful in this world.
These people were unable to celebrate
The happiness of others
And sought only their own happiness.
Even worse,
Those who attained happiness
Or sought their own happiness by sacrificing others
Are also suffering in hell.

This shows
There are voices of resentment
Of those who suffered to make them successful
While alive.
The thought waves of pain and suffering of those
Who became the sacrifice for their success while alive
Are making them suffer like that in hell.
No, it may be more accurate to say
The fact that they made many people suffer
And caused them grief while alive
Was brought back to the memories of their souls,
Urging the souls to reap their own karma now.
This is how the world of the mind works.
While living on earth,
Their senses were dulled
Because they resided in a physical body,
So perhaps they were not aware
Of other people's feelings.
But while having a physical body,
If they were as sensitive
As they are after leaving this world,
Then they would have felt such a hell while being alive.
They would have felt such vibrations of hell.

However,
Some people suffer like that for the first time
When they return to the other world
Decades after that.
But no one can laugh at them
Because there is a high possibility
That the very people who laugh at them will
Eventually end up the same.

You must tell people on earth as well.
Those who succeed in this world
Will not necessarily return to the higher realms of heaven.
High status in this world does not necessarily indicate
A high status in the other world.
Rather, the higher your status is in this world,
The stronger the pain you will feel when fallen.
You must know this.
Of course, the heavenly world is a wonderful world.
Heaven, too, certainly differs
According to each individual's state of mind.
Even so,
Compared to the world of hell,
Heaven is wonderful everywhere.

It will not be difficult
Especially for those who lived rightly with a pure mind
To be welcomed into a world of peace.
They will quite naturally return to the world
That is filled with peace and joy.
On the other hand,
Those who were in the whirlpools
Of worries and sufferings
And could not wipe them out while in this world
Will continue to agonize over them in the other world.

Indeed, that is why,
As the first condition of enlightenment,
You must be determined
To not bring your worries and sufferings with you
When you return to the other world.
To put it another way,
You must clear your delusions,
Put an end to your worries,
And overcome your sufferings
Now, here, in this lifetime.
The world of worry awaits
Those who have left this world with worries.

The world of agony awaits
Those who have left this world with agony.
The world of sorrow awaits
Those who have left this world with sorrow.
However,
It is the world of joy that awaits
Those who have left this world with joy.

The Gospel of Hope

Therefore, all of you, my disciples,
First, put the teachings of Buddha
At the center of your learning.
Make Buddha's teachings
The pillar of your learning.
Always study Buddha's teachings,
Always absorb them into your minds,
And live rightly every day by learning them.
Living rightly every day
Is more important than anything.
At that time, do not make a mistake:
You must control your minds

Using the knowledge of Buddha's Truth.
Always remember to govern your minds
Using the knowledge of Buddha's Truth.
Always remember to rule over yourselves
Using the knowledge of Buddha's Truth.
Knowledge will serve to control emotions.
Most of your mistakes lie in your emotions,
Your feelings, and your thoughts.
These are where your mistakes lie.
What controls them
Is the correct knowledge of Buddha's Truth.
You must control your thoughts and emotions
Using the correct knowledge of Buddha's Truth.

All of you, my disciples,
Even so, you have the gospel of hope.
Rejoice that there is the gospel of hope.
It means that
Not a single thing you have learned in this lifetime
Will go to waste.
Sometimes what you have learned in this life
May not serve anything in this lifetime.
However, what you have learned in this life

Will surely stand you in good stead in the future,
In your next life, and in your life after that.
After leaving this world,
You will live for hundreds of years or even longer
In the Real World.
And when your souls want to go
For the next training,
You will be born on earth with a physical body,
Taking on a new appearance.
That is to say,
You will be born as a baby,
Grow up, and live through various worries again.
However, what you have gained
Through the soul training in this lifetime
Will definitely stand you in good stead
In the soul training in your next life.
It will definitely be useful in the next life's soul training
And guide you in a good direction.
This being so,
What you have gained in this lifetime
Is not the merit of this lifetime alone.
It will go beyond this lifetime
And will surely make you happy in your next life

And in the life after that.
Therefore,
Even if you have suffered through making efforts
During the period of your soul training,
Do not make them your suffering.

What you have achieved
Is not the achievement of this lifetime alone.
It will become a power
To change your souls fundamentally.
It will serve as spiritual training
For your souls to gain power fundamentally.
Since you are undergoing
Such precious spiritual training,
You must never feel daunted.
Do you know the power of the mind?
Do you know the power of spiritual training?
Even when you feel you have run out of energy now,
If you persevere and continue to work hard,
The power hidden within
Will gush forth more and more.
Your power is limitless,
For you are endowed with Buddha-nature.

When the power of this Buddha-nature
Manifests itself,
Its energy is infinite;
Its light is infinite.
When you are advancing toward Buddha,
You shall never tire.
You shall never be weary.
You shall never be hurt.
Even if you worry, suffer, get tired, and become weary
As you learn and spread Buddha's teachings
In this world,
You, who have kept on building up those efforts,
Will surely be taken to the land of Light and Peace
After leaving this world.
It is not long before this happens.
It will be in just some decades
Or just some years.
Why not live for these teachings during that time?
Why not abide by these teachings during that time?
Why not keep your souls burning to the fullest
Under these teachings during that time?

All of you, from now on,
Abide by these Laws of Truth,

And make efforts every day.
The teachings of Buddha will taste better
As you chew on them more and more,
As you listen to them more and more.
And as you practice them more and more,
The fragrance of enlightenment will spread
All around you.
You must know the true taste of enlightenment.
You may be simply reading my books,
Or you may be simply listening to my teachings,
But if they do not truly nourish your souls,
Then you are just the same as the silver spoon
That does not know the taste of the soup,
No matter how much it scoops.
You must become a person
Who can enjoy the taste of enlightenment.
You must become a person
Who can smell the fragrance of enlightenment.
You must become a person
Who can hear and distinguish
The melodies of enlightenment.
When you can do these,
You can be called for the first time
A true practitioner of spiritual training.

You will find the path to enlightenment
Opening before you.

CHAPTER SEVEN

Faith and the Road
to Creating Buddha Land

All of you, my disciples,
Now let me finally talk about faith.

What Are Buddha and God?

Many of you probably have faith.
However,
Do you fully grasp the real meaning of faith?
Of course,
Faith is your strong will toward Buddha or God.
There is no faith without such a will.
But do you really understand the real nature of
Buddha or God that people should worship?
Because there are various religions in the world
And each religion has its own gods with different names,
People may find it hard to decide what to believe in.
I think this is the current situation.

However, all of you, my disciples,
Sometimes this cannot be helped.
That is because Buddha—

The Grand Spirit of the great universe—
Is a far grander, greater Being;
It is beyond human understanding.
The Buddha, or God, that you can understand
Is no more than the Spirit you can perceive
Through your physical bodies,
Your spiritual knowledge,
And your perception.
However, you probably understand that
There is a world far beyond your recognition.
Indeed, there is a power
That is beyond your recognition.
This power contains wisdom.
This power contains light.
This power contains love.
This power is filled with mercy.
This power is filled with constructive thoughts.
This power is filled with beautiful harmony.
The power that incorporates
Everything that is considered good—
That is the power of Buddha.

You may also not understand
The difference between Buddha and God.
Some may think there is no need
To explain the difference between the two.
You may simply think that
Buddhists use the word "Buddha,"
While other religions,
Including Christianity and Japanese Shinto,
Have the concept, "God."
However, I must at least tell you this.
It is true that
Among those that are called "Buddha" or "God"
Are the so-called high spirits,
Or personified gods, or personified buddhas.
Some may call them "Buddha" while others "God,"
But they are indeed referring to "high spirits."
However, it is also true that
There is a Being that transcends high spirits.
At least, it can be said that
High spirits are the ones
Who have been born on earth
With a physical body in the past.
But Buddha, who created Heaven and Earth

And who created the great universe,
Never dwells in a small human body
To undergo soul training.
In this sense, it is true that
There is a Grand Consciousness
That far transcends the human character.

In a way,
This kind of explanation
May weaken your power to believe.
However, please listen to me carefully.
To know the truth
Is an act to fill yourselves with power.
By knowing the truth,
Your convictions will be stronger,
And you will come to have
An even greater spirit of devotion.

Feeling Gratitude to the Grand Spirit of the Great Universe

For this reason,
First, your faith must be directed at Buddha,
Who governs the great universe.
It must be directed
At this Grand Spiritual Consciousness
That governs the great universe.
It must be directed
At this Integrating Cosmic Consciousness
That governs the great universe.
But this Grand Spirit of the great universe
Does not grant your wishes
Or give answers to your problems
Because It does not possess human character.
It is Buddha that just gives away love, light,
And energy to you,
Just like the sun.
Therefore, to this Ultimate Buddha,
Express your faith through "gratitude."
Live each day with gratitude.
Dedicate gratitude to Buddha,

The Great Nurturer who created the great universe
And allows all beings to live,
This Grand Spirit of the great universe—
This is the mission of human beings living on earth.
I believe so.

Revering High Spirits

But then there are highly advanced high spirits
Who teach you, guide you, love you,
And give answers to your problems
In concrete forms.
You have probably learned these contents
In many ways.
It is actually natural that
These high spirits make their appearances
In various forms.
Just as modern people have heard about
People of great character
Who transcend time and region,
Living in various parts of the world,
Many high spirits of the Real World

Left their names in history.
Of course,
Even these high spirits reside in different places.
Some are close to the Ultimate, to Buddha,
While others are relatively closer to human beings.

In this way,
High spirits reside in different dimensions
Depending on the individual.
Their living spaces are different.
We must accept these differences.
Although there are clear differences,
We nevertheless cannot deny that
These high spirits who are sometimes called "gods"
Are all great beings.
These great beings—or rather, their wisdom—
Are beyond reach for anyone living on earth,
No matter how wise the person may be.
You must understand this.
For this reason,
First, show your respect.
Be respectful to them.

Such a respectful attitude is naturally required.
I think so.

I told you to express your faith through gratitude
To the ultimate Grand Spirit of the great universe.
To high spirits,
You must express your faith through a respectful attitude,
Not to mention gratitude.
What exactly is this attitude?
It means to be in awe.
It means to revere.
Feeling awe and revering those in higher dimensions,
Those with greater virtue,
Those with abundant leadership,
Abundant love, and abundant mercy—
You must never forget these.
Even in this world,
It is difficult to talk to someone
Of a different status directly.
In the same way,
In the world far beyond this one, too,
There are beings who transcend

The soul training of humans on earth.
To all such beings,
You must show the utmost respect.
I believe so.

That is because this is a rule.
That is because the Beings called
The "great personified spirits"
Were once the Parents of the souls of humans on earth.
That is because they were the Parents of the souls
And the Teachers of the souls.
You must have deep, deep gratitude
To these teachers of the souls.
The work of the teachers of the souls
Is not limited to this lifetime alone.
Through repeated incarnations in the past,
The teachers of the souls have definitely taught you
Many things.
Because the teachers of the souls have taught you
Many things,
You are now living happily;
You are now living without going astray.
What is more,

You are now able to live with deep faith
Because the high spirits have guided you
In the process of many incarnations in the past.
To such guidance, you must show your sincere respect.
I believe so.

The Foundation of Faith

Now, so far, I told you that
You have to show your respect in two directions.
One is the respect toward
The Grand Spirit of the great universe,
Who should be called Primordial God
Or Primordial Buddha of the universe;
The other is the respect toward high spirits.
To put it another way,
Your faith must be fundamentally based on
The attitude of devotion to the great beings,
The attitude of devotion to those with wisdom,
The attitude of devotion to those with power,
Those with light, those with great wisdom,
And those with love.

When they give you and you are given
And when you receive guidance,
You definitely need to have such an attitude.

The difference between those who are called high spirits
And humans on earth is vast.
They are almost as different as elephants and ants.
Despite that,
An ant is trying to judge an entire elephant.
I can only say it is truly ludicrous.
Just imagine.
How can an ant assess an entire elephant?
Can an ant understand who he is?
That would be really difficult.
In the same way,
It is difficult for humans on earth
To assess great high spirits.
That is because they cannot recognize
The entire picture of the high spirits.
However,
If you look deeply into your minds,
You will surely feel something.
Religions give various teachings,

Be it Buddhism, Christianity, or any other religious sect.
But what they teach probably resonates with you
Deep in your souls,
Making you feel
You have learned these teachings somewhere before.
Yes, that must be true.
When you read the teachings of Buddhism
Or the teachings of Christianity,
Perhaps your souls feel nostalgic for some reason;
You understand these teachings for some reason.
The words of the past leaders of Light,
Born in different ages and regions,
Are now understood by you
After transcending thousands of years of history
And moving your souls.
This is a fact.
What do you think of it?
Is it strange to you?
Or do you see it as a matter of course?

Indeed, it is nothing strange.
Those high spirits who gave teachings
In different regions and in different ages

Are now in the Real World,
Guarding and guiding you again.
Under this great power,
You have now come together
And are now learning the Laws.

Devoting Yourself to Buddha

And yet I leave you the following words.
You must have faith in the Primordial Grand Spirit,
Who created the universe,
And pay respect to
The great high spirits of the Real World
Residing in the heavenly world beyond this one.
And there is yet another Being you must pay respect to.

That is the Buddha who is born on earth.
The Buddha is not sacred merely for His existence.
He is sacred
Because He is granted the Power,
Enlightenment, Light, Love, and Mercy
By the great Grand Spirit.

Even if you devote yourselves
To the Primordial Buddha of the universe,
Even if you devote yourselves
To the high spirits of the Real World,
If you do not have the spirit of devotion
To the Buddha who has descended on earth,
Your faith is fake.
That is because all those who formerly taught
The great religions in the world
Are awakened ones, enlightened ones,
And buddhas who descended on earth.
If not through the people of such a position,
It would not be possible to bring down Buddha's voice,
Buddha's philosophies, and Buddha's ideals on earth.

For this reason,
The Primordial Buddha of the great universe,
The high spirits of the Real World,
And the Buddha descended on earth form a Trinity;
They are all sacred beings.
Faith will not be born
If there is no feeling of equally revering
These three Beings.

Some may create their own image
Of the Primordial Buddha of the great universe
According to their own preference
And think of specific spirits of the Real World
To have faith in.
But if they defile the teachings of the Buddha on earth
And defy His teachings,
Then they are going against
The Will of the Grand Spirit of the great universe.
That is because the Grand Spirit of the great universe
Entrusts the Buddha with all responsibilities of His age;
It is because the Buddha descends on earth
With all authority.
The One who determines the value judgment in the age,
The One who determines what is right in the age,
The One who determines what is good in the age,
And the One who determines
What is truth in the age—
That is the Buddha.
That is why
No matter how much you respect in your mind
Someone of the past,
No matter how much you respect in your mind

Buddha or God that presumably dwells far away
In the universe,
If you do not have any respect for the Buddha
Who has descended on earth,
Then you are no longer a person with faith.
You are no longer a person on the Path.
You are no longer a person seeking the Path.
In this way,
Seekers of the Path must know their places.

Those mindless people will later have regret
In the hundreds or thousands of years to come.
Many people did not believe that Christ was there
Despite living in the time of Jesus.
The very people who did not believe that
Christ was there
Were later reborn on earth after
Hundreds or thousands of years
And now believe in the Crucifixion of Jesus in church.
Do not repeat such a folly.
When the Awakened One is on earth,
Be sure to have faith in Him.
When the Awakened One is on earth,

Be sure to rejoice in being born in the same age as Him.
You must be in awe of His authority.
You must believe in His authority.
You must submit to His authority.
Those who deny and loathe His authority
Or those who try to understand this authority
Within their limited awareness
Shall all be tossed into the abyss of fallacy.
It is the same as denying Buddha of the universe.
It is the same as blaspheming against
Buddha of the universe.
Sending a representative of Buddha onto earth
Is a unanimous idea of
The personified Grand Spirits in heaven.
So when a representative of Buddha descends on earth,
Making everything in accord with His ideas
Is the right thing to do.
This is the foundation of faith.
I say this again and again.

Hundred Percent Faith

Therefore,
The Laws will be taught
Only when people have the attitude
Of devotion to the Buddha on earth.
Without this attitude,
The true Laws will not be taught.
The true Laws will not be taught in doubt.
What expands in doubt is the domain of devils.
In all ages, devils sneak into people's doubts.
They sneak into people's doubts
And cause them to disagree with each other.
They cause people to speak nonsense to each other,
Making them fall out,
And eventually tear them apart.
They try to tear down people's faith.
They try to disturb the minds of believers.
O people, however,
Never be deluded.
You must never be deluded.
What can you understand with your small brains?
What can you know

By just understanding with your small brains?
What can you understand with your petty intellect?
How can you possibly weigh
The Great Wisdom of Buddha
With such small brains,
With such petty intellect?
How can you possibly have insights
Into the Will of the personified Grand Spirit
Who sent the Buddha onto earth?
Laugh at the pettiness of yourselves.
Humble yourselves for your own smallness.
Know that you do not stand in such a position.
Doubt is the mind of devils.
Skepticism, too, is the mind of devils.
Fear, too, is the mind of devils.
These minds cannot be called the exploring mind.
Those who study Buddha's Truth
Need to have the attitude to explore things.
But the attitude to explore things
Is not the attitude to be skeptical.
The exploring mind is neither a skeptical mind
Nor a doubtful mind.
Should these minds arise in you,

You are no longer on the path of spiritual training.
At that time,
You can no longer be called
A practitioner of spiritual training.

O you, who practice spiritual training,
All of you, my disciples,
If anyone among you has doubts in faith,
Isolate yourself silently
And wait until your mind becomes peaceful.
Wait for that time.
Never speak any words of criticism.
Calm your mind silently and reflect on your life.
Be grateful for how much light,
How much love you have been given.
You must not raise doubts recklessly
Or delude other people's minds recklessly
Without feeling such gratitude.
Know that such thoughts and actions
Lie at the closest to hell.
Even if you have served the Buddha,
Protected the Laws well, and guided others for 40 years,
If you doubt the Buddha's Laws,

Disrupt the Laws,
And delude people's minds in the final year,
You shall surely fall to hell.
This is how faith is.
Faith must be 100 percent;
There is no such thing as 99-percent faith.
The 99-percent faith is the same as no faith at all.
Faith demands 100 percent devotion.
For Buddha is everything.
Because Buddha is everything,
Unless you believe in Him 100 percent,
You cannot gain everything.
Even if you have lived 99 years of your life in faith,
If you lived the last year of your life
As a mistaken materialist,
Then you shall surely fall to hell.
You must know that
There is such a strict side to faith.

The Sin of Disrupting the Harmony of Disciples

The sin of deluding and disrupting
The people who have entered the Path and
Are practicing spiritual training
Is especially deadly.
This is called
"The sin of disrupting the harmony of disciples."
Some join the group of people
Who have come under Buddha's Truth,
Practice spiritual training, and live in faith together,
But they commit the sin of taking people's faiths away,
Casting doubts in their minds,
And disrupting the group.
These people have committed
The sin of disrupting the harmony of disciples.
It is difficult to be exempt from this sin.
This sin, this extremely great sin, is so serious
That even murder, robbery, or assault is no match.
Murder is merely separating souls
From their physical bodies on earth.
Assault is merely inflicting pain

On physical bodies on earth.
However, those who delude
People practicing spiritual training
And living with the right mind
Are committing the sin of
Tormenting other people's minds,
Making other people's souls rot,
And making them deluded.
This sin is deadly.
Those who take away people's faith and delude them
Shall wait for the time of self-refection in hell for long.
You must never commit such a sin.

Seek the Path with Humility

Now I have taught you many things about faith.
All of you, my disciples,
Do you think
This kind of faith is no longer appealing
In the modern age?
Do you think it is out-of-date?
However, I say to you:

Buddha's Truth is timeless.
Buddha's Truth transcends time.
Buddha's Truth shines brightly beyond ages.
The most important part of Buddha's Truth
Is the same in every age,
And nothing can trample on it.
Nothing can ignore it.
What was true in the age of Shakyamuni Buddha
Held true in the age of Jesus Christ.
And it holds true in this modern age as well.
You must know this.
The basis of Buddha's philosophy never changes.
So you must know that
You are still only a small being.
You must know that
You are still only an immature being.
You must know that
You are still only a person
Who must seek the Path with humility.
Never, ever become conceited.
Conceit is the most terrifying enemy
For those practicing spiritual training.
In the face of the enemy of conceit,

If you cannot defeat it,
All the spiritual training you have undergone
Will immediately come to nothing.
Your spiritual training will evaporate overnight.
O practitioners of spiritual training,
Therefore, fear conceit the most.
Be wary of conceit the most.
Perceive conceit as your greatest enemy.
Conceit is the mind to indulge yourselves.
It is the mind to spoil yourselves.
It is the mind to want to have your own way.
It is the mind of how you want to be.
When you think to your advantage
And desire to be a certain way,
Devils will come down to you
And whisper words that sound nice to you.
If you come to believe in these words,
You will gradually move away from the true Laws.
You must not be conceited.
You must be strict with yourselves.
Be strict on yourselves.
And always be humble.
Do not become arrogant.

Do not become too proud.
Always remember to devote yourselves to your Master.
Always remember to revere your Master.
And move forward steadily with humility,
One step at a time.
This is the path
Of faithful practitioners of spiritual training.

Even at the Cost of Your Life

All of you, my disciples,
Now I have taught you the importance of faith.
In any age, faith is important.
Should you ever face the decision
Of choosing between your life and your faith,
Choose faith without hesitation.
If you choose faith,
You shall not lose your eternal lives forever.
You shall find yourselves in eternal glory.
However, if you choose earthly life
When urged to choose between earthly life and faith,
You will tremendously agonize over the choice you made

After leaving this world.
After having continued spiritual training
With such strong determination
And with such strong will,
You ended up abandoning the path of faith
Because of such an easy temptation.
This fact will be retained as a disgraceful shame
For hundreds or thousands of years
After leaving this world.
The bitter feeling of your soul will know no end.
Such bitterness of the soul is so intense
That you would say it was better
To have your body being torn apart by a saw
While on earth.
When the great Buddha descended on earth in the past,
Some people lost faith in Him
And committed sins against their Master.
Do you know how much pain their souls have felt
And the agonizing lives they led after leaving this world?
So losing faith is more serious than losing a life on earth.
Even if you should lose your life,
Do not lose your faith.
Do not let go of your faith for position, fame, money,

Or lust toward the opposite sex.
There will be a time in your lives
When you waver
And think hard about which to choose.
If you work for a company, for example,
You may value a position or honor.
If you are a person of social standing,
You may also value fame.
You may also value money.
You may value the love of your wife or husband.
However, no matter what you put on a scale,
Know that nothing weighs more than faith.
Faith is to be directly united with Buddha.
Faith is to be directly connected to Buddha.
Faith is to become one with Buddha.
Know that there is nothing in this world
That weighs more than Buddha.
No matter what you place on a scale—
Any earthly things, be it gold, silver,
Or any other treasures—
Nothing is heavier than Buddha.
Faith is to be one with Buddha.
Never forget this oneness with Buddha.

Without such faith,
It is impossible to create Buddha Land.
I believe so.

Without Faith...

I am sure many of you are passionate
About the ideal of creating Buddha Land.
The creation of Buddha Land in this ideal
Is by no means a worldly or superficial Buddha Land.
Buddha Land is Buddha Land
Because it is the land Buddha approves,
Because it is the world Buddha thinks is ideal.
That is the condition of true Buddha Land.
Then, what do you have to do
To create the land Buddha approves
And the society Buddha approves?
There is no doubt that it must be based on faith.
So if you are to create Buddha Land in the country of Japan,
All Japanese people must awaken to faith.
If you want to spread this Buddha Land
To regions beyond Japan,
If you want to create Buddha Land in Southeast Asia,

South Korea, China, America, Europe, India,
And various other countries and regions,
You must firmly establish faith as a foundation
In each country.
Without faith, all things are barren.
Only when you receive an education based on faith
Can you acquire culture for the first time.
Without the basis of faith,
No matter how much you cram yourselves
With academic learning,
You can never be truly cultured.
Such a culture is fake.
It is a mere collection of scientific knowledge,
Or materialistic knowledge
That denies the existence of Buddha.
It cannot be called true culture.
True culture is only built upon the foundation of faith.
True culture is created only based on faith,
Filling the earth with truly cultured people,
And there manifests a peaceful world.

All of you,
This is the undeniable Truth
That exists in all ages.

If you are to create Buddha Land,
First, you must fill that country or region
With wonderful people.
The wonderful people who must fill the region
Are those who have faith at their basis.
No matter how many people may fill the nation,
If they do not believe in Buddha,
That nation will never become Buddha Land.
First, you must nurture the people
Who believe in Buddha
And who have the right faith.
As a matter of course,
Parents must teach faith to their children.
This is the greatest duty of parents.
This is the greatest education parents can give.
I believe so.
Being a parent,
If you neglect this education,
What other important education can there be?
There is no such education.
It is nothing but the sheer negligence of the parent's duty.
O fathers of the world,
O mothers of the world,

Many of you may ask
What is necessary for educating your children.
But I dare say to you:
Without faith, any education will be barren.
Without belief in Buddha,
Any education will be barren.
It will bear no crops.
It will bear no fruits.
On the contrary,
It will only produce
People who scatter bad things to the world.
If you want to obtain good crops,
First, till the land.
Tilling the land is essential.
Till the land, and sow good seeds.
Once you sow good seeds, fertilize the soil well.
And water it well.
Then, your crops will grow big, bearing much fruit.

Begin at Home

In faith,
Good soil is necessary first.
Good soil means a harmonious home.
It is essential that
Both husband and wife are overflowing with faith
And are filled with harmony.
In such a harmonious home,
Good seeds shall bear fruit.
That is to say,
Wonderful children will be raised.
When bringing up children,
Do not forget to water and fertilize them.
Water is something indispensable;
It is the courage to live.
Fertilizer is the words of Buddha's Truth or wisdom;
It is the words of wisdom.
Teach children the words of Buddha's Truth,
The words of wisdom,
And give them the courage to live
And the hope to live.
Then, children will grow up healthy
And eventually become capable people in society.

In this way,
The creation of Utopia or the creation of Buddha Land
Must begin at home.
Creating Buddha Land from home
Is the most important thing.
This is because
Even a population of a hundred million people
Can be broken down into family units
Of just four or five people.
Even if it is difficult to align
The entire hundred million people
With the spirit of creating Buddha Land Utopia,
It is easy to create Buddha Land Utopia
In a family of four or five people.
This is the basis of all things.
First, you must begin with small things.
Only after creating Utopia at home
Can a society become Utopia,
Can a nation become Utopia.
This is how things are.

So, all of you, my disciples,
Listen carefully to my following words.
First, you must not neglect your family.

Engrave in your hearts
That the creation of Buddha Land is impossible
If you neglect your family.
In negligence of your own family,
Even if you do charitable work outside,
Even if you provide refugee relief outside,
Even if you donate money outside,
No matter how pious your acts may be,
If you neglect your family,
Your faith is not true.
Buddha's Truth always begins with your surroundings.
Without turning where you live, where you are,
And your own home into Utopia first,
You cannot turn the entire world into Utopia.
Remember this well.
Who can make your home into Utopia?
Do you think someone will come
And make your home into Utopia?
When you abandon your responsibilities at home
And disturb the harmony of your family,
How can you expect a complete stranger
To come into your home
And turn everything into Utopia?

Such a thing never happens.
You are the one creating disharmony in the family.
No, everyone in your family is responsible.
If so, start by creating Utopia from within yourselves.

I also say to many of the women of today.
You have forgotten the most important work.
As I have just said,
To make this world Utopia,
First you need to create Utopia at home.
This is a mission given by Buddha.
Even if you are successful in society
And are working to make the entire world a Utopia,
You can never achieve it
If you have abandoned creating Utopia at home.
Remember, it is in no way desirable
In the eyes of Buddha.
From now on, know that
Those who neglect their families
Do not deserve to practice spiritual training.
Those who practice spiritual training
Must first cherish their families.
Those with a wife must cherish the wife,

Those with a husband must cherish the husband,
Those with children must cherish the children,
And those with parents must cherish the parents.
Unless you value the harmony of your family in this way,
You do not deserve to truly practice spiritual training
As a seeker of Truth, in the first place.
You must understand this.
So I say to the many women of today:
No matter how much worldly recognition you may earn,
No matter how much worldly success you may achieve,
And no matter how much savings you may have,
If you have broken your family
And destroyed your household,
I must say these deeds of yours
Will be all connected to hell.
Truly.
Buddha's teachings always lie there.
O many of the women,
Is making Utopia at home
Such a shameful thing to do?
Is making your home into Buddha Land
Such a lowly work for you?
If you do not do this work, who else will?

Do not wander about in cities as if feeling tipsy,
Neglecting this sacred mission,
Being swept by frivolous trends of the world,
And being deluded by
Unimportant words and opinions of the world.
Never, ever neglect your home.

From the Mind to the World

Each person harmonizing their own family—
This is the basis of all Utopia.
Utopia is not possible without this.
I will say this to you.
This actually makes up 90 percent of
The work of creating Utopia.
If you are to make this world a Buddha Land,
Ninety percent of your work
Is in the creation of Utopia at home.
Only after achieving this 90 percent of the work
Will there be Utopia as a whole.
The remaining work is only 10 percent.
The remaining 10 percent of the work

Is the next challenge:
How the entire society, or the entire nation,
Plays the role of filling itself with harmony and prosperity.
But if everyone succeeds in creating Utopia at home,
How can a society fail to work?
How can a nation fail to work?
Only when everyone sheds the light
Filled with harmony
Will the world be a better place for the first time.
When all complaints and dissatisfaction disappear
From each home,
I wonder what difficult problems there can be in a nation.
Maybe just unnecessary doubts.
Maybe just needless worries.
Yes, ultimately,
The nation does not necessarily need work.
If groups of utopian families exist,
Then that is everything.
That is the kind of world we must aim for as an ideal.
We must discard as much as possible
The idea of Utopia being realized by
Someone else's power,
Through someone else's intervention.

You must stick to the small starting point
And think about ways to make the whole world a Utopia
By starting from your own mind.
This is the unchanging, imperishable,
And everlasting Law in all ages.
This is the Eternal Law.
Engrave this deep, deep into your mind.
Be absolutely sure not to forget this.

Afterword (Original Edition)

This book has an extremely unique style compared with the other books I have written so far.

First, this book takes the form of a message to my disciples—that is, to monks and nuns undergoing spiritual training or, in modern terms, to all men and women who practice spiritual training.

Some parts of my message may sound quite demanding, but the path of Buddha's Truth that I teach you is indeed very steep. You can never reach the summit of the mountain of Buddha's Truth with a half-hearted attitude.

Therefore, I think it is possible to read this book in two ways. One is for those of you who have already entered the path of Buddha's Truth: a warning to show that your life will be this severe. The other is for those of you who still hesitate to stand at the gate of Buddha's Truth: a good textbook or introduction to show how far you have to go.

In either case, I am sure that by reading this book, you will see that here lies the true heart of Shakyamuni Buddha.

I sincerely wish that you will savor the spiritual power of these words again and again.

Ryuho Okawa
Master & CEO of Happy Science Group
July 1989

Afterword to the New Edition

My disciples, be strong.

Conquer all worldly temptations and wrong views, and gather to me.

You need to have the indomitable resolve to hear the direct message of Buddha given from his Golden Mouth. The udumbara flower only blooms once every 3,000 years. And it is agreed that only one Buddha is born into one age.

"Now, gather to the Buddha Reborn!"—Upon this calling, all Light of Bodhisattvas shall come together.

Ryuho Okawa
Master & CEO of Happy Science Group
October 1994

ABOUT THE AUTHOR

Founder and CEO of Happy Science Group.

Ryuho Okawa was born on July 7th 1956, in Tokushima, Japan. After graduating from the University of Tokyo with a law degree, he joined a Tokyo-based trading house. While working at its New York headquarters, he studied international finance at the Graduate Center of the City University of New York. In 1981, he attained Great Enlightenment and became aware that he is El Cantare with a mission to bring salvation to all humankind.

In 1986, he established Happy Science. It now has members in over 165 countries across the world, with more than 700 branches and temples as well as 10,000 missionary houses around the world.

He has given over 3,400 lectures (of which more than 150 are in English) and published over 3,000 books (of which more than 600 are Spiritual Interview Series), and many are translated into 40 languages. Along with *The Laws of the Sun* and *The Laws Of Messiah*, many of the books have become best sellers or million sellers. To date, Happy Science has produced 25 movies. The original story and original concept were given by the Executive Producer Ryuho Okawa. He has also composed music and written lyrics of over 450 pieces.

Moreover, he is the Founder of Happy Science University and Happy Science Academy (Junior and Senior High School), Founder and President of the Happiness Realization Party, Founder and Honorary Headmaster of Happy Science Institute of Government and Management, Founder of IRH Press Co., Ltd., and the Chairperson of NEW STAR PRODUCTION Co., Ltd. and ARI Production Co., Ltd.

WHAT IS EL CANTARE?

El Cantare means "the Light of the Earth," and is the Supreme God of the Earth who has been guiding humankind since the beginning of Genesis. He is whom Jesus called Father and Muhammad called Allah, and is *Ame-no-Mioya-Gami*, Japanese Father God. Different parts of El Cantare's core consciousness have descended to Earth in the past, once as Alpha and another as Elohim. His branch spirits, such as Shakyamuni Buddha and Hermes, have descended to Earth many times and helped to flourish many civilizations. To unite various religions and to integrate various fields of study in order to build a new civilization on Earth, a part of the core consciousness has descended to Earth as Master Ryuho Okawa.

Alpha is a part of the core consciousness of El Cantare who descended to Earth around 330 million years ago. Alpha preached Earth's Truths to harmonize and unify Earth-born humans and space people who came from other planets.

Elohim is a part of the core consciousness of El Cantare who descended to Earth around 150 million years ago. He gave wisdom, mainly on the differences of light and darkness, good and evil.

Ame-no-Mioya-Gami (Japanese Father God) is the Creator God and the Father God who appears in the ancient literature, *Hotsuma Tsutae*. It is believed that He descended on the foothills of Mt. Fuji about 30,000 years ago and built the Fuji dynasty, which is the root of the Japanese civilization. With justice as the central pillar, Ame-no-Mioya-Gami's teachings spread to ancient civilizations of other countries in the world.

Shakyamuni Buddha was born as a prince into the Shakya Clan in India around 2,600 years ago. When he was 29 years old, he renounced the world and sought enlightenment. He later attained Great Enlightenment and founded Buddhism.

Hermes is one of the 12 Olympian gods in Greek mythology, but the spiritual Truth is that he taught the teachings of love and progress around 4,300 years ago that became the origin of the current Western civilization. He is a hero that truly existed.

Ophealis was born in Greece around 6,500 years ago and was the leader who took an expedition to as far as Egypt. He is the God of miracles, prosperity, and arts, and is known as Osiris in the Egyptian mythology.

Rient Arl Croud was born as a king of the ancient Incan Empire around 7,000 years ago and taught about the mysteries of the mind. In the heavenly world, he is responsible for the interactions that take place between various planets.

Thoth was an almighty leader who built the golden age of the Atlantic civilization around 12,000 years ago. In the Egyptian mythology, he is known as god Thoth.

Ra Mu was a leader who built the golden age of the civilization of Mu around 17,000 years ago. As a religious leader and a politician, he ruled by uniting religion and politics.

BOOKS BY RYUHO OKAWA

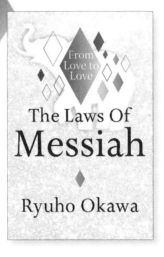

The Laws Of Messiah
From Love to Love

Paperback • 248 pages • $16.95
ISBN: 978-1-942125-90-7 (Jan. 31, 2022)

"What is Messiah?" This book carries an important message of love and guidance to people living now from the Modern-Day Messiah or the Modern-Day Savior. It also reveals the secret of Shambhala, the spiritual center of Earth, as well as the truth that this spiritual center is currently in danger of perishing and what we can do to protect this sacred place.

Love your Lord God. Know that those who don't know love don't know God. Discover the true love of God and the ideal practice of faith. This book teaches the most important element we must not lose sight of as we go through our soul training on this planet Earth.

THE ESSENCE OF BUDDHA

THE PATH TO ENLIGHTENMENT

Paperback • 208 pages • $14.95
ISBN: 978-1-942125-06-8 (Oct.1, 2016)

In this book, Ryuho Okawa imparts in simple and accessible language his wisdom about the essence of Shakyamuni Buddha's philosophy of life and enlightenment–teachings that have been inspiring people all over the world for over 2,500 years. By offering a new perspective on core Buddhist thoughts that have long been cloaked in mystique, Okawa brings these teachings to life for modern people. *The Essence of Buddha* distills a way of life that anyone can practice to achieve a life of self-growth, compassionate living, and true happiness.

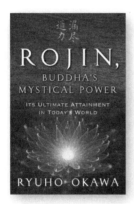

ROJIN, BUDDHA'S MYSTICAL POWER

ITS ULTIMATE ATTAINMENT IN TODAY'S WORLD

Paperback • 232 pages • $16.95
ISBN: 978-1-942125-82-2 (Sep. 24, 2021)

In this book, Ryuho Okawa has redefined the traditional Buddhist term *Rojin* and explained that in modern society it means the following: the ability for individuals with great spiritual powers to live in the world as people with common sense while using their abilities to the optimal level. This book will unravel the mystery of the mind and lead you to the path to enlightenment.

THE TRUE EIGHTFOLD PATH

GUIDEPOSTS FOR SELF-INNOVATION

Paperback • 272 pages • $16.95
ISBN: 978-1-942125-80-8 (Mar. 30, 2021)

This book explains how we can apply the Eightfold Path, one of the main pillars of Shakyamuni Buddha's teachings, as everyday guideposts in the modern-age to achieve self-innovation to live better and make positive changes in these uncertain times.

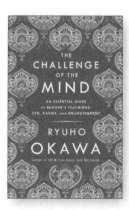

THE CHALLENGE OF THE MIND

AN ESSENTIAL GUIDE TO BUDDHA'S TEACHINGS: ZEN, KARMA AND ENLIGHTENMENT

Paperback • 208 pages • $16.95
ISBN: 978-1-942125-45-7 (Nov. 15, 2018)

In this book, Ryuho Okawa explains essential Buddhist tenets and how to put them into practice. Enlightenment is not just an abstract idea but one that everyone can experience to some extent. Okawa offers a solid basis of reason and intellectual understanding to Buddhist concepts. By applying these basic principles to our lives, we can direct our minds to higher ideals and create a bright future for ourselves and others.

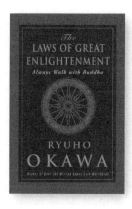

THE LAWS OF GREAT ENLIGHTENMENT

ALWAYS WALK WITH BUDDHA

Paperback • 232 pages • $17.95
ISBN: 978-1-942125-62-4 (Nov. 7, 2019)

Constant self-blame for mistakes, setbacks, or failures and feelings of unforgivingness toward others are hard to overcome. Through the power of enlightenment we can learn to forgive ourselves and others, overcome life's problems, and courageously create a brighter future ourselves. *The Laws of Great Enlightenment* addresses the core problems of life that people often struggle with and offers advice on how to overcome them based on spiritual truths.

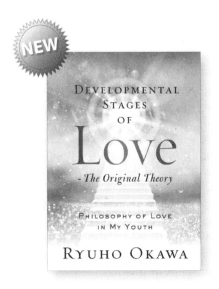

DEVELOPMENTAL STAGES OF LOVE
- THE ORIGINAL THEORY

PHILOSOPHY OF LOVE IN MY YOUTH

Hardcover • 200 pages • $17.95
ISBN: 978-1-942125-94-5 (Jun. 15, 2022)

This book is about author Ryuho Okawa's original philosophy of love which serves as the foundation of love in the chapter three of *The Laws of the Sun*. It consists of series of short essays authored during his age of 25 through 28 while he was working as a young promising business elite at an international trading company after attaining the Great Enlightenment in 1981. This revolutionary philosophy, developmental states of love, is the idea to unite love and enlightenment, West and East, and bridges Christianity and Buddhism. It is also the starting point of the global utopian movement, Happy Science.

THE TEN PRINCIPLES FROM EL CANTARE VOLUME I

RYUHO OKAWA'S FIRST LECTURES ON HIS BASIC TEACHINGS

Paperback • 232 pages • $16.95
ISBN: 978-1-942125-85-3 (Dec. 15, 2021)

This book contains the historic lectures given on the first five principles of the Ten Principles of Happy Science from the author, Ryuho Okawa, who is revered as World Teacher. These lectures produced an enthusiastic fellowship in Happy Science Japan and became the foundation of the current global utopian movement. You can learn the essence of Okawa's teachings and the secret behind the rapid growth of the Happy Science movement in simple language.

THE TEN PRINCIPLES FROM EL CANTARE VOLUME II

RYUHO OKAWA'S FIRST LECTURES ON HIS WISH TO SAVE THE WORLD

Paperback • 216 pages • $16.95
ISBN: 978-1-942125-86-0 (May. 3, 2022)

A sequel to *The Ten Principles from El Cantare Volume I*. Volume II reveals the Creator's three major inventions; the secret of the creation of human souls, the meaning of time, and 'happiness' as life's purpose. By reading this book, you can not only improve yourself but learn how to make differences in society and create an ideal, utopian world.

EL CANTARE TRILOGY BY RYUHO OKAWA

The Laws Series is an annual volume of books that are comprised of Ryuho Okawa's lectures that function as universal guidance to all people. They are of various topics that were given in accordance with the changes that each year brings. *The Laws of the Sun*, the first publication of the laws series, ranked in the annual best-selling list in Japan in 1994. Since, the laws series' titles have ranked in the annual best-selling list every year for more than two decades, setting socio-cultural trends in Japan and around the world.

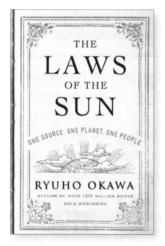

THE LAWS OF THE SUN

ONE SOURCE, ONE PLANET,
ONE PEOPLE

Paperback • 288 pages • $15.95
ISBN: 978-1-942125-43-3 (Oct. 15, 2018)

IMAGINE IF YOU COULD ASK GOD why He created this world and what spiritual laws He used to shape us—and everything around us. If we could understand His designs and intentions, we could discover what our goals in life should be and whether our actions move us closer to those goals or farther away.

At a young age, a spiritual calling prompted Ryuho Okawa to outline what he innately understood to be universal truths for all humankind. In *The Laws of the Sun*, Okawa outlines these laws of the universe and provides a road map for living one's life with greater purpose and meaning. In this powerful book, Ryuho Okawa reveals the transcendent nature of consciousness and the secrets of our multidimensional universe and our place in it. By understanding the different stages of love and following the Buddhist Eightfold Path, he believes we can speed up our eternal process of development. *The Laws of the Sun* shows the way to realize true happiness—a happiness that continues from this world through the other.

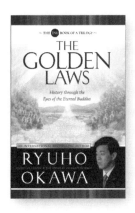

THE GOLDEN LAWS

HISTORY THROUGH THE EYES OF THE ETERNAL BUDDHA

Paperback • 201 pages • $14.95
ISBN: 978-1-941779-81-1 (Jul. 1, 2011)

Throughout history, Great Guiding Spirits have been present on Earth in both the East and the West at crucial points in human history to further our spiritual development. *The Golden Laws* reveals how Divine Plan has been unfolding on Earth, and outlines 5,000 years of the secret history of humankind. Once we understand the true course of history, through past, present and into the future, we cannot help but become aware of the significance of our spiritual mission in the present age.

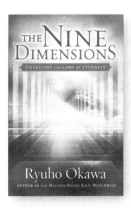

THE NINE DIMENSIONS

UNVEILING THE LAWS OF ETERNITY

Paperback • 168 pages • $15.95
ISBN: 978-0-982698-56-3 (Feb. 16, 2012)

This book is a window into the mind of our loving God, who designed this world and the vast, wondrous world of our afterlife as a school with many levels through which our souls learn and grow. When the religions and cultures of the world discover the truth of their common spiritual origin, they will be inspired to accept their differences, come together under faith in God, and build an era of harmony and peaceful progress on Earth.

AUTHOR'S STORY (TIMELESS WISDOM)

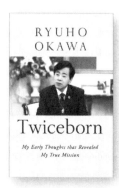

TWICEBORN

MY EARLY THOUGHTS THAT REVEALED
MY TRUE MISSION

Hardcover • 206 pages • $19.95
ISBN: 978-1-942125-74-7 (Oct. 7, 2020)

This semi-autobiography of Ryuho Okawa reveals the origins of his thoughts and how he made up his mind to establish Happy Science to spread the Truth to the world. It also contains the very first grand lecture where he declared himself as El Cantare. The timeless wisdom in *Twiceborn* will surely inspire you and help you fulfill your mission in this lifetime.

THE NEW RESURRECTION

MY MIRACULOUS STORY OF
OVERCOMING ILLNESS AND DEATH

Hardcover • 224 pages • $19.95
ISBN: 978-1-942125-64-8 (Feb. 26, 2020)

The New Resurrection is an autobiographical account of an astonishing miracle experienced by author Ryuho Okawa in 2004. This event was adapted into the feature-length film *Immortal Hero*. Today, Okawa lives each day with the readiness to die for the Truth and has dedicated his life to selflessly guiding faith seekers towards spiritual development and happiness.

HOW TO BECOME A CREATIVE PERSON

Paperback • 176 pages • $16.95
ISBN: 978-1-942125-84-6 (Oct. 15, 2021)

How can we become creative when we feel we are not naturally creative? This book provides easy to follow universal and hands-on-rules to become a creative person in work and life. These methods of becoming creative are certain to bring you success in work and life. Discover the secret ingredient for becoming truly creative.

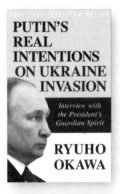

PUTIN'S REAL INTENTIONS ON UKRAINE INVASION

INTERVIEW WITH THE PRESIDENT'S GUARDIAN SPIRIT

Paperback • $13.95 • ISBN: 978-1-943928-32-3
E-book • $12.99 • ISBN: 978-1-943928-33-0

Why did Russia invade Ukraine? The author and spiritual leader Ryuho Okawa conducted a spiritual interview with the guardian spirit of President Vladimir Putin in order to provide sources for the world to understand the top leader's thoughts and to make future judgements and predictions. The true nature of the Russia-Ukraine conflict and Putin's thoughts is here.

THE DESCENT OF JAPANESE FATHER GOD AME-NO-MIOYA-GAMI

THE "GOD OF CREATION" IN THE ANCIENT DOCUMENT HOTSUMA TSUTAE

Paperback • $14.95 • ISBN: 978-1-943928-29-3
E-book • $13.99 • ISBN: 978-1-943928-31-6

By reading this book, you can find the origin of bushido (samurai spirit) and understand how the ancient Japanese civilization influenced other countries. Now that the world is in confusion, Japan is expected to awaken to its true origin and courageously rise to bring justice to the world.

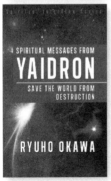

SPIRITUAL MESSAGES FROM YAIDRON SAVE THE WORLD FROM DESTRUCTION

Paperback • $11.95 • ISBN: 978-1-943928-23-1
E-book • $10.99 • ISBN: 978-1-943928-25-5

In this book, Yaidron explains what was going on behind the military coup in Myanmar and Taliban's control over Afghanistan. He also warns of the imminent danger approaching Taiwan. According to what he observes from the universe, World War III has already begun on Earth. What is now going on is a battle between democratic values and the communist one-party control. How to overcome this battle and create peace on Earth depends on the faith and righteous actions of each one of us.

TRUTH ABOUT LIFE, DEATH AND AFTERLIFE

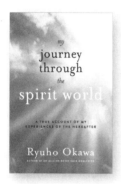

MY JOURNEY THROUGH THE SPIRIT WORLD

A TRUE ACCOUNT OF MY EXPERIENCES OF THE HEREAFTER

Paperback • 224 pages • $15.95
ISBN: 978-1-942125-41-9 (Jul. 25, 2018)

What happens when we die? Do heaven and hell really exist? This book reveals surprising facts such as that we visit the spirit world during sleep and that people continue to live in the same lifestyle as they did in this world. This unique and authentic guide to the spirit world will awaken us to the truth of life and death, and show us how we can return to a bright world of heaven.

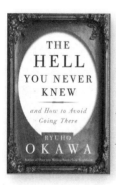

THE HELL YOU NEVER KNEW

AND HOW TO AVOID GOING THERE

Paperback • 192 pages • $15.95
ISBN: 978-1-942125-52-5 (Jul. 15, 2019)

From ancient times, people have been warned of the danger of falling to Hell. But does the world of Hell truly exist? If it does, what kind of people would go there? Through his spiritual abilities, Ryuho Okawa found out that Hell is only a small part of the vast Spirit World, yet more than half of the people today go there after they die.

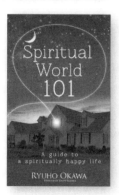

SPIRITUAL WORLD 101

A GUIDE TO A SPIRITUALLY HAPPY LIFE

Paperback • $14.95 • ISBN: 978-1-941779-43-9
E-book • $13.99 • ISBN: 978-1-941779-45-3

This book is a spiritual guidebook that will answer all your questions about the spiritual world, with illustrations and diagrams explaining about your guardian spirit and the secrets of God and Buddha. By reading this book, you will be able to understand the true meaning of life and find happiness in everyday life.

OTHER RECOMMENDED TITLES

THE LAWS OF SECRET
Awaken to This New World and Change Your Life

THE LAWS OF FAITH
One World Beyond Differences

THE LAWS OF MISSION
Essential Truths for Spiritual Awakening in a Secular Age

THE MOMENT OF TRUTH
Become a Living Angel Today

THE LAWS OF JUSTICE
How We Can Solve World Conflicts and Bring Peace

THE ROYAL ROAD OF LIFE
Beginning Your Path of Inner Peace, Virtue, and a Life of Purpose

THE POSSESSION
Know the Ghost Condition and Overcome
Negative Spiritual Influence

THE LAWS OF STEEL
Living a Life of Resilience, Confidence and Prosperity

THE REAL EXORCIST
Attain Wisdom to Conquer Evil

For a complete list of books, visit <u>okawabooks.com</u>

MUSIC BY RYUHO OKAWA

El Cantare Ryuho Okawa Original Songs

____ A song celebrating ____
Lord God

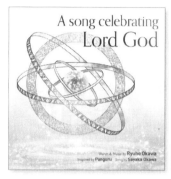

A song celebrating Lord God,
the God of the Earth,
who is beyond a prophet.

DVD
CD

─── The Water Revolution ───
English and Chinese version

For the truth and happiness of the
1.4 billion people in China who
have no freedom. Love, justice,
and sacred rage of God are on this
melody that will give you courage
to fight to bring peace.

DVD

CD

Search on YouTube

the water revolution for a short ad!

Listen now today!

 Download from
Spotify **iTunes** **Amazon**

DVD, CD available at amazon.com,
and Happy Science locations worldwide

ABOUT HAPPY SCIENCE

Happy Science is a global movement that empowers individuals to find purpose and spiritual happiness and to share that happiness with their families, societies, and the world. With more than 12 million members around the world, Happy Science aims to increase awareness of spiritual truths and expand our capacity for love, compassion, and joy so that together we can create the kind of world we all wish to live in.

Activities at Happy Science are based on the Principles of Happiness (Love, Wisdom, Self-Reflection, and Progress). These principles embrace worldwide philosophies and beliefs, transcending boundaries of culture and religions.

Love teaches us to give ourselves freely without expecting anything in return; it encompasses giving, nurturing, and forgiving.

Wisdom leads us to the insights of spiritual truths, and opens us to the true meaning of life and the Will of God (the universe, the highest power, Buddha).

Self-Reflection brings a mindful, nonjudgmental lens to our thoughts and actions to help us find our truest selves—the essence of our souls—and deepen our connection to the highest power. It helps us attain a clean and peaceful mind and leads us to the right life path.

Progress emphasizes the positive, dynamic aspects of our spiritual growth—actions we can take to manifest and spread happiness around the world. It's a path that not only expands our soul growth, but also furthers the collective potential of the world we live in.

PROGRAMS AND EVENTS

The doors of Happy Science are open to all. We offer a variety of programs and events, including self-exploration and self-growth programs, spiritual seminars, meditation and contemplation sessions, study groups, and book events.

Our programs are designed to:

* Deepen your understanding of your purpose and meaning in life
* Improve your relationships and increase your capacity to love unconditionally
* Attain peace of mind, decrease anxiety and stress, and feel positive
* Gain deeper insights and a broader perspective on the world
* Learn how to overcome life's challenges
  ... and much more.

For more information, visit <u>happy-science.org</u>.

CONTACT INFORMATION

Happy Science is a worldwide organization with branches and temples around the globe. For a comprehensive list, visit the worldwide directory at *happy-science.org*. The following are some of the many Happy Science locations:

UNITED STATES AND CANADA

New York
79 Franklin St., New York, NY 10013, USA
Phone: 1-212-343-7972
Fax: 1-212-343-7973
Email: ny@happy-science.org
Website: happyscience-usa.org

New Jersey
66 Hudson St., #2R, Hoboken, NJ 07030, USA
Phone: 1-201-313-0127
Email: nj@happy-science.org
Website: happyscience-usa.org

Chicago
2300 Barrington Rd., Suite #400, Hoffman Estates, IL 60169, USA
Phone: 1-630-937-3077
Email: chicago@happy-science.org
Website: happyscience-usa.org

Florida
5208 8th St., Zephyrhills, FL 33542, USA
Phone: 1-813-715-0000
Fax: 1-813-715-0010
Email: florida@happy-science.org
Website: happyscience-usa.org

Atlanta
1874 Piedmont Ave., NE Suite 360-C
Atlanta, GA 30324, USA
Phone: 1-404-892-7770
Email: atlanta@happy-science.org
Website: happyscience-usa.org

San Francisco
525 Clinton St. Redwood City, CA 94062, USA
Phone & Fax: 1-650-363-2777
Email: sf@happy-science.org
Website: happyscience-usa.org

Los Angeles
1590 E. Del Mar Blvd., Pasadena, CA 91106, USA
Phone: 1-626-395-7775
Fax: 1-626-395-7776
Email: la@happy-science.org
Website: happyscience-usa.org

Orange County
16541 Gothard St. Suite 104
Huntington Beach, CA 92647
Phone: 1-714-659-1501
Email: oc@happy-science.org
Website: happyscience-usa.org

San Diego
7841 Balboa Ave. Suite #202
San Diego, CA 92111, USA
Phone: 1-626-395-7775
Fax: 1-626-395-7776
E-mail: sandiego@happy-science.org
Website: happyscience-usa.org

Hawaii
Phone: 1-808-591-9772
Fax: 1-808-591-9776
Email: hi@happy-science.org
Website: happyscience-usa.org

Kauai
3343 Kanakolu Street, Suite 5
Lihue, HI 96766, USA
Phone: 1-808-822-7007
Fax: 1-808-822-6007
Email: kauai-hi@happy-science.org
Website: happyscience-usa.org

Toronto
845 The Queensway Etobicoke,
ON M8Z 1N6, Canada
Phone: 1-416-901-3747
Email: toronto@happy-science.org
Website: happy-science.ca

Vancouver
#201-2607 East 49th Avenue,
Vancouver, BC, V5S 1J9, Canada
Phone: 1-604-437-7735
Fax: 1-604-437-7764
Email: vancouver@happy-science.org
Website: happy-science.ca

INTERNATIONAL

Tokyo
1-6-7 Togoshi, Shinagawa,
Tokyo, 142-0041, Japan
Phone: 81-3-6384-5770
Fax: 81-3-6384-5776
Email: tokyo@happy-science.org
Website: happy-science.org

Seoul
74, Sadang-ro 27-gil, Dongjak-gu,
Seoul, Korea
Phone: 82-2-3478-8777
Fax: 82-2-3478-9777
Email: korea@happy-science.org
Website: happyscience-korea.org

London
3 Margaret St.London,
W1W 8RE United Kingdom
Phone: 44-20-7323-9255
Fax: 44-20-7323-9344
Email: eu@happy-science.org
Website: www.happyscience-uk.org

Taipei
No. 89, Lane 155, Dunhua N. Road,
Songshan District, Taipei City 105, Taiwan
Phone: 886-2-2719-9377
Fax: 886-2-2719-5570
Email: taiwan@happy-science.org
Website: happyscience-tw.org

Sydney
516 Pacific Highway, Lane Cove North,
2066 NSW, Australia
Phone: 61-2-9411-2877
Fax: 61-2-9411-2822
Email: sydney@happy-science.org

Kuala Lumpur
No 22A, Block 2, Jalil Link Jalan Jalil Jaya
2, Bukit Jalil 57000,
Kuala Lumpur, Malaysia
Phone: 60-3-8998-7877
Fax: 60-3-8998-7977
Email: malaysia@happy-science.org
Website: happyscience.org.my

Sao Paulo
Rua. Domingos de Morais 1154,
Vila Mariana, Sao Paulo SP
CEP 04010-100, Brazil
Phone: 55-11-5088-3800
Email: sp@happy-science.org
Website: happyscience.com.br

Kathmandu
Kathmandu Metropolitan City,
Ward No. 15, Ring Road, Kimdol,
Sitapaila Kathmandu, Nepal
Phone: 977-1-427-2931
Email: nepal@happy-science.org

Jundiai
Rua Congo, 447, Jd. Bonfiglioli
Jundiai-CEP, 13207-340, Brazil
Phone: 55-11-4587-5952
Email: jundiai@happy-science.org

Kampala
Plot 877 Rubaga Road, Kampala
P.O. Box 34130 Kampala, UGANDA
Phone: 256-79-4682-121
Email: uganda@happy-science.org

ABOUT HAPPINESS REALIZATION PARTY

The Happiness Realization Party (HRP) was founded in May 2009 by Master Ryuho Okawa as part of the Happy Science Group. HRP strives to improve the Japanese society, based on three basic political principles of "freedom, democracy, and faith," and let Japan promote individual and public happiness from Asia to the world as a leader nation.

1) Diplomacy and Security: Protecting Freedom, Democracy, and Faith of Japan and the World from China's Totalitarianism

Japan's current defense system is insufficient against China's expanding hegemony and the threat of North Korea's nuclear missiles. Japan, as the leader of Asia, must strengthen its defense power and promote strategic diplomacy together with the nations which share the values of freedom, democracy, and faith. Further, HRP aims to realize world peace under the leadership of Japan, the nation with the spirit of religious tolerance.

2) Economy: Early economic recovery through utilizing the "wisdom of the private sector"

Economy has been damaged severely by the novel coronavirus originated in China. Many companies have been forced into bankruptcy or out of business. What is needed for economic recovery now is not subsidies and regulations by the government, but policies which can utilize the "wisdom of the private sector."

For more information, visit en.hr-party.jp

HAPPY SCIENCE ACADEMY
JUNIOR AND SENIOR HIGH SCHOOL

Happy Science Academy Junior and Senior High School is a boarding school founded with the goal of educating the future leaders of the world who can have a big vision, persevere, and take on new challenges.

Currently, there are two campuses in Japan; the Nasu Main Campus in Tochigi Prefecture, founded in 2010, and the Kansai Campus in Shiga Prefecture, founded in 2013.

Nasu Main Campus

Kansai Campus

HAPPY SCIENCE UNIVERSITY

THE FOUNDING SPIRIT AND THE GOAL OF EDUCATION

Based on the founding philosophy of the university, "Exploration of happiness and the creation of a new civilization," education, research and studies will be provided to help students acquire deep understanding grounded in religious belief and advanced expertise with the objectives of producing "great talents of virtue" who can contribute in a broad-ranging way to serving Japan and the international society.